For Gera

W9-CQS-820

Sincerely,

Muriel Gardiner

Code Name "Mary"

Code Name "Mary"

Memoirs of an American Woman in the Austrian Underground

MURIEL GARDINER

Yale University Press
New Haven and London

Designed by Nancy Ovedovitz and set in Trump Medieval
type by Waldman Graphics. Printed in the United States of
America by Murray Printing Company, Westford, Mass.

Library of Congress Cataloging in Publication Data
Gardiner, Muriel, 1901–
    Code name "Mary"
    1. Austria—Politics and government—1918–1938.
    2. Austria—Politics and government—1938–1945.
    3. Gardiner, Muriel, 1901– . 4. Americans—Austria
—Biography. I. Title.
DB97.G37 1983   943.6′051′0924   82–20213
ISBN 0–300–02940–3

10   9   8   7   6   5   4   3   2   1

For Joe and Connie

Contents

Illustrations

Foreword

by Anna Freud

Man-made catastrophes such as wars, revolutions, perse-cutions, hijackings, etc., not only reveal what is worst in human nature; in some people at least, they also release what is best.

The author of this book was not the only visitor from abroad who enjoyed the deceptive peace of Austria in the early 1930s. Like many others, she appreciated the beauties and amenities of Vienna, the easily formed friendships, the sense of privacy and seclusion provided by the glens, mead-ows, and forests adjacent to the city.

Also, like many others of her compatriots, she was caught up inadvertently in the political troubles which swept through Central Europe. However, she belonged to neither the hunt-ers nor the hunted, the persecutors nor the persecuted. The ugly scenes which followed Hitler's triumphant entry into Austria need have been none of her concern. Prudence, as well as the protection of her young daughter, would have advised that she follow the example of the many other Americans who did not hesitate to return to their native country, in her case to the safe, comfortable, and luxurious background which the book describes so well.

Nevertheless, and in the face of all reason, she remained, apparently with the aim of finishing her medical studies, but even more to help her friend's political collaborators.

And from these, her helpfulness and compassion began to spread: to their friends; to the friends of friends; to anybody in trouble, however remote and unfamiliar; until she was surrounded by a whole crowd of potential victims who looked to her as possibly their only hope of salvation.

Those of us who, at this period, were forced to share the experience of lying sleepless in bed in the early morning hours, waiting for the dreaded knock of the Gestapo at our doors, find it difficult, even impossible, to imagine that anybody could choose voluntarily to face the same anxieties. Every hidden socialist or Jew searched for and found in Muriel Gardiner's apartment would have meant the end, not only for him but also for her; every trip to the border escorting refugees or carrying their photographs, every return bringing false passports, could have ended in disaster. And this was not all. There were all the other accompaniments of an underground existence: the inevitable failures; the disappearances which placed people beyond the possibility of help; the endlessly drawn-out waiting periods when nothing happened; the discomforts and deprivations of daily life; the frightening possibility of being duped by impostors and the humiliating experience of being taken for an impostor herself.

There are other and fuller accounts of the happenings of this period, recording the struggle and disorganization of the Social Democratic party of Austria or the plight of its Jewish population or the exact number of individuals driven into exile, deported, or exterminated. The present book does not aspire to belong to their category. It is a rendering of personal experiences, an attempt to depict how history affects the lives of individuals, and it should be read for its descriptions of individual despair, of the tearing apart and attempted reunion of families, of the search for countries of refuge, the battle for life-saving affidavits, and the neverending planning and plotting which, often enough, had to be abandoned again as unrealistic and impossible to carry into action.

What are harsh realities at one moment in time may dwindle to distant nightmares forty years later. However, that is no reason to relegate them to oblivion. The present generation of readers, even if far removed from such experience, may welcome two lessons which can be learned from it: one, that it is possible even for lone individuals to pit their strength successfully against the sinister forces of an unjust regime; and, two, that for every gang of evil-doers who take pleasure in hurting, harming, and destroying, there is always at least one "just" man or woman ready to help, rescue, and sacrifice his or her own good for fellow-beings.

Introduction

Soon after Lillian Hellman's book *Pentimento* appeared in 1973, friends and acquaintances of mine began telephoning me, saying, "Muriel, you must be 'Julia.' " Or my Austrian friends here who still call me by my underground code name would say, "Mary, you have to be 'Julia.' " After receiving a few dozen such calls, some even from people who did not know me but knew refugees I had helped, I read the Hellman story and was indeed struck by the many similarities between my life and her heroine's. I have never met Lillian Hellman but had often heard about her from a friend with whose family we shared a large house in New Jersey for more than ten years. I had known this friend since the late 1920s, and he had visited me once in Vienna. I knew of his great interest in theater, of his friendships with many actors, actresses, producers, and playwrights, and I enjoyed hearing his stories of these interesting people.

After the film *Julia* appeared, many more people began asking me about my life, even addressing me as "Julia." On my next visit to Vienna, I asked Dr. Herbert Steiner, director of the Documentation Archives of the Austrian Resistance, what other American women he knew of who had been deeply involved in the Austrian anti-Fascist or anti-Nazi underground. He knew of none. Some months later Dr. Steiner wrote me that since our talk he had renewed contact with many former resistance workers to ask them about American women they had known or heard of who were deeply involved in the resistance. Their answer was always: "Only Mary."

Long before I had heard of "Julia," I was attempting to write my autobiography. My husband, Joseph Buttinger, was already engaged in writing his and wanted me to write mine also, so that we could intertwine the two, chapter by chapter. Many friends had urged us to do this, finding it interesting that two persons with such completely contrasting backgrounds—geographical, educational, religious, financial, and in many other respects—had met at about age thirty, fighting for the same cause and with almost identical ideals and values, and have lived together harmoniously for more than forty years.

I made several autobiographical attempts, but none of them satisfied me. I was inhibited by feelings of privacy and by my training—as a psychoanalyst, physician, and educator—in keeping confidences. I was simply unable to write openly about many important aspects of my life. At length I decided to confine myself to the period in which I was actively involved in the anti-Fascist and anti-Nazi struggle, namely from February 1934 in Vienna until leaving Paris in the fall of 1939, after the outbreak of the Second World War. This period was, I think, the one of greatest general interest in my life, and there was little during this time that I could not write about openly after so many years. One dear and wise friend, after reading the following chapters, advised me against publishing them in the first person, feeling that "I" should everywhere be changed to "she." Although this appealed to me in one way, in another it did not seem quite natural or quite honest. I decided I would rather risk lack of modesty than questionable honesty.

One

Early Years:
My Life until February 1934

I was at my psychoanalytic session with Dr. Ruth Mack Brunswick at her home in The Hasenauerstrasse, in Vienna's eighteenth district, on Monday, February 12, 1934, when the shooting began. Army units and police of Dollfuss's Fascist government had begun to attack the large apartment buildings where they suspected armed members of the Socialist Defense League were assembled. The Hasenauerstrasse was not far from some of these workers' homes, and we could hear the guns distinctly. When, moments later, we heard the tat-tat-tat of the machine guns quite close, Dr. Brunswick, putting reality and human concern ahead of any principles of analytic technique, told me that we would break off the hour and that she would ask her chauffeur to drive me home. As usual, I had traveled the several miles from my apartment to Dr. Brunswick's by streetcar, but we both assumed that the threatened general strike had broken out; the streetcars would not be running, and to walk would be hazardous. Grateful for Dr. Brunswick's suggestion, I took my place beside her chauffeur in the car. Already police and soldiers stood with machine guns on many corners and military vehicles were in the streets. The streetcars had indeed stopped and been emptied; there were few civilians or ci-

1

vilian vehicles to be seen. I remember the day as being dark
and cold—but this might be only because of the eerie atmosphere of impending doom, like that created by a beginning eclipse of the sun.

Even during this short drive, and certainly during the following days, I could not help contrasting these scenes—and,
above all, my feelings—with those I had experienced when
the Fascists marched into Rome in October 1922. Returning
by bus from an expedition on that brilliant, sunny Saturday
afternoon, I and other students of the American School of
Classical Studies were stopped at the gates of Rome by armed
Fascist soldiers and barbed wire. Although at twenty I had
already been involved in political issues for several years
and was a determined anti-Fascist, I did not take Mussolini
and his Fascists very seriously and thought it rather a lark
to be halted at the Porta Flaminia. The other students were
even less involved than I, and we laughed and joked while
the director of the expedition dickered with the Fascist guards
until the barbed wire was finally rolled back and we were
allowed to proceed into the city. There the streets were
swarming with Fascisti and civilians, laughing and singing,
"Giovinezza, giovinezza, primavera di bellezza, il Fascismo
è la salvezza della nostra libertà" ("Youth, youth, spring-
time of beauty, Fascism is the salvation of our liberty"). It
all seemed rather ridiculous to me. Even that night when,
looking out our pension windows in the Piazza dell'Esquilino,
we saw men shooting and others running for cover, when
people shouted up to us, "Close your windows!," I had had
none of the ominous, heart-sinking feelings I had on this
February day in Vienna, more than eleven years later. Was
this because of the difference in character between the Ital-
ians and the Austrians? Or because I had scarcely known
Italy, but had made Vienna my home for more than six
years? Or because I was now more politically sophisticated
and knew I was living in a world headed toward disaster?
Or was it just the difference between being thirty-two and

being twenty? I believe it was something of each of these, and of many less tangible factors, too.

I knew at once, in February 1934, that the brave Socialist resistance to Dollfuss and the Austrian Fascists was doomed; and in fact it lasted only a few days. Coffins of those who had died fighting for Dollfuss, draped with the Austrian red-white-red flag, were lined up in the Rathausplatz and finally carried away on open, horse-drawn wagons, to the funeral march of Beethoven's *Eroica*.

As I stood in the Rathausplatz, tremendously moved by the coffins and the solemn, heroic music, pity and despair overwhelmed me. But they could not cancel out the feelings that had been building up within me these past few days: indignation, anger, and an imperative need to continue the struggle, hopeless though it might be.

Since graduating from Wellesley twelve years earlier, I had been involved in travel, study, archaeology, music, medicine, psychoanalysis, and my personal life. Interested as always in world events and politics, and fond of discussing them with my friends, I had nevertheless gradually withdrawn from political activities. This was partly because there seemed nothing a private American citizen living in Europe could do and partly because of my conviction that a second world war was building up and that nothing could be done to stop it. I even kept a scrapbook of clippings to this effect. Without any conscious decision to do so, I had simply "dropped out." (The single exception was the Sacco-Vanzetti case, in which I had been passionately involved from the beginning in 1920 until the execution of the two men in 1927, doing the few things an individual could do: writing letters, signing petitions, making contributions, attending meetings when in America.) Though not submissive at heart, I had become a sorrowful bystander while great national and international events unrolled.

The events of February 1934 changed this passive attitude into an urgent need for activity. Again there was no con-

scious decision on my part. The change this time was not
gradual but sudden; it took place within the few days of the
fighting, perhaps even within the first hours or minutes.
The first thing to be done, when life had returned to "normal," was to find ways to help the wounded and the endangered still in hiding. I did not expect this to be easy. I had
few really intimate friends in Vienna at the time, and there
was not a single politically involved Austrian among them.
But there were several English friends who were aware of
my political leanings and had contacts with Austrian Socialists as well as with English and American journalists.
Two or three of them asked if they might give my name to
some involved friends, and someone gave me an introduction to a sympathetic journalist, G. E. R. Gedye, who could
put me in touch with people in the underground. Almost
immediately a considerable number of persons contacted
me.

Someone would telephone me rather furtively and give
me a clue as to how he had gotten my name. We would set
a time—often that same evening—and the person, man or
woman, would come to my apartment. Occasionally he would
give me his name; more often there were no introductions
or he would say: "When I call you again, I'll announce myself as Hans." The immediate need was for money. I found
myself in an embarrassing situation. I could not judge which
of these persons were the more reliable and the more efficient or who was in contact with those most in need. I had
no way of controlling to whom the money would be passed
or how it would be used. I did not know who was a Socialist,
who a Communist. At this stage it did not matter too much,
as I was willing to aid all resisters as best I could; but I soon
became a little wary of some of the intermediaries. They
wanted to know much more about me than they would
divulge about themselves. Their secrecy was natural and
commendable, yet their talk and behavior were sometimes
indiscreet. I was at a loss as to how to direct my efforts and

how to judge the merits of the diverse people and their appeals.

Otto Bauer, leader of the Social Democratic party, Julius Deutsch, head of the Socialist Defense League, a few other well-known figures, and many members of the Defense League had been able to leave Austria secretly during or just after the fighting. They went to Brno (also called Brünn) in Czechoslovakia, only about seventy-five miles from Vienna. (Czechoslovakia was at that time still a free, independent country.) The most prominent Socialists still remaining in Vienna, including Otto Leichter and Oskar Pollak, editors of the *Arbeiter-Zeitung* (Workers' Newspaper), tried to become inconspicuous and called themselves a "Shadow Committee." However, they sought out and helped to organize others into a Central Committee with which they could secretly remain in touch and retain their influence. It was important to keep the party alive by distributing information and literature illegally printed in Austria or brought in from Brno, where Bauer, still considered party leader, and other comrades in exile had control of the party funds. The Social Democrats had been declared illegal. Later in 1934, when the conservative Vaterländische Front (Fatherland Front) was established, all other political parties, including the Nazis, had been abolished. I knew little of party details at the time, and none of the people involved. My first task, it seemed to me, was to get help to the February victims still in Vienna.

In my search for some person or group I could work with seriously, I met Leopold and Ilse Kulczar. At first I was reticent with them, but as we talked I became impressed by their intelligence and their political wisdom. They were leftist Socialists who, having belonged to the Communist party for several years, and then left it, were politically knowledgeable and experienced. The Kulczars, who had an apartment in the Hochhaus, one of the more modern buildings in the center of Vienna, were organizing a group of the underground, which came to be called the Funke, or Spark group, after Lenin's Iskra. At this point the Kulczars were the only persons I had met who seemed to me to know how the underground movement should be organized and what precautions must be taken. I very soon felt I could identify my goals and plans with theirs. At the same time, I was a little distrustful of their characters. I could not help forming impressions of people by what I saw in their faces. In Ilse's face I thought I saw selfishness, in Poldi's a tendency to deceit and perhaps ruthlessness if it served his purpose. I tried not to judge by these impressions; I knew I might well be wrong. Even if I were right, these qualities might not necessarily interfere with their work.

Poldi visited me several times, trying to enlist my services as well as money in their secret organization. He spoke in a rather grandiose way of a large number of five-person cells the Funke group had organized for discussion and resistance work. He described a system of transporting underground literature into Austria from Czechoslovakia. He taught me many of the rules of conspiracy. We all had code names; for myself I chose "Mary." Before I agreed to help, I told Poldi I wanted to visit one of the underground cells. He took me, one warm spring evening, to a basement apartment in Floridsdorf, where there were indeed four or five young people gathered around a table. We joined them, Poldi acting as leader of the cell. One young man, with the cover-name "Hermann," was or became a member of the Funke Central Committee. I later got to know him well. Except for Poldi, he was the only member of this cell with whom I had further close contact. I heard no more about the cells and came to suspect that the seventy-five Poldi had spoken of were merely a dream.

As I became more involved with the Kulczars, I grew more cautious about other political contacts but did not drop them all. Once "the little Otto Bauer," so called to distinguish him from the exiled Socialist leader of the same name, came to my apartment with a few other people. Bauer belonged to the League of Religious Socialists. I saw him only this one time in 1934 but later he became a close friend. Before summer I had broken off contact with most of the persons whose names I did not know. Through English friends I met young Hugh Gaitskell, later a British Labour party leader and Chancellor of the Exchequer, and saw him often as long as he remained in Vienna. We had many good talks, usually combined with an excursion in the Vienna Woods, sometimes with other friends. I occasionally saw the British journalist G. E. R. Gedye,* who had helped me make contact with the underground. I always learned much from him.

My commitment to anti-Fascism and my resolve to actively oppose the Fascist movement were the beginning of all that became the core of my life for the next six or more years and has remained an essential part of my thinking, feeling, my very self ever since. This is perhaps the moment to try to explain how an American woman studying psychoanalysis and medicine in Vienna came to identify herself so closely with Socialists and the Austrian workers. It was not a sudden metamorphosis, although it may have seemed so to my family and even to some of my friends. With little knowledge but strong feelings, I had had leanings in this direction before I was ten years old. I must begin at the beginning.

I was born in Chicago on November 23, 1901, the last child in a family of two boys and two considerably younger girls. My father, Edward Morris, was the eldest son of Nelson Morris, the founder of Morris & Company, one of the first and largest meat-processing firms in Chicago. Grandfather Morris, a Jewish boy whose former name was Beisinger, at age thirteen had come alone from Hechingen, in southern Germany, to the United States (with one dollar in his pocket, we had always been told), during the waves of

*Gedye later wrote a book about this period called *Fallen Bastions* (London: V. Gollancz, Ltd., 1939).

immigration from central Europe in the years following 1848. He landed at Philadelphia, where he was picked up at the dock by a farmer seeking cheap labor. After a year with the farmer, who did not treat him well, Nelson Morris ran away and gradually made his way westward to Chicago.

At twenty-three my father, who had already worked at Morris & Company for a number of years, married Helen Swift, the daughter of Gustavus Swift, founder of Swift & Company, another of the great Chicago meat-packing firms. All my mother's ancestors, originally of English stock, were from New England. Mother was four years old when her family left their home on Cape Cod and traveled west, living in several different villages or towns until they finally settled in Chicago. Grandfather Swift, after founding Swift & Company, was often referred to as "the Yankee of the yards." Both my grandfathers had been poor as youngsters, but both had become very rich by the time I came into the world.

My grandfather Morris died when I was five, and my father—the only member of his family in the business—ran the firm until his early death in 1913. After that my brothers took over, with considerable help, I am sure, from my mother, a good businesswoman, until they sold Morris & Company to Armour in the early 1920s.

So I grew up the child of rich parents, with my own yearly allowance from age twelve and an independent income after age twenty-one. We lived on Chicago's South Side in great luxury, first in an imposing castlelike house of brown granite, with lawns and stables and a huge play-yard. When I was ten my parents built us a still larger house, in late Tudor style, which, with its gardens, garage, stables, and tennis court, occupied half a large city block. We had more than a dozen servants: a housekeeper, a cook, a laundress, my mother's maid, my father's valet, our nurse, a gardener, a coachman-chauffeur, two butlers, and several maids.

Although our material wants were luxuriously provided for and we were given every educational opportunity, I do not think that we were "spoiled" in other respects. Both my

parents—my mother from a strict puritanical background—
had high ethical standards, believed in hard work, and were
themselves extremely well disciplined. They demanded
complete obedience from us, truthfulness, fairness, and po-
liteness. Their insistence on discipline and obedience, although valuable training which I appreciated more as I grew
older, had its reverse side also. I was afraid of my mother
and father and never that I can remember confided in either
of them. I was seldom untruthful but became adept in con-
cealing everything I knew they would disapprove of. I speak
of "them," but actually I had little contact with my father,
who worked from early until late every day except occasional Saturday afternoons and Sundays and brief vacations
in summer.

The person I loved most was Mollie, our nurse, who had
been with us since the birth of my oldest brother and remained until I went to college. She was a warm, comforting
person, and the only way she ever "punished" us was by her
occasional threat: "I'll have to tell your mother." As I grew
older I felt very sad that I could not love my mother as I
loved Mollie. I admired my mother and felt sorry for her. I
dearly loved my brother Nelson, ten years older than I, a
person of rare kindness and generosity who was constantly
thinking of ways to give his sisters pleasure. Among other
things, Nelson was, from an early age, a skilled conjurer,
and he always entertained us as magician at our children's
parties, at the end of his act producing the traditional white
rabbit out of an empty hat, to the astonished delight of all.
(Later he performed elegantly at benefits on shipboard and
elsewhere.) Edward, a year younger than Nelson, was lively,
full of fun, a practical joker, and a great tease. His teasing,
especially tickling, often amounted to torment for me, his
chosen object, but we were expected to be "good sports,"
and I suppose neither he nor my parents realized what a
torture this was. Ruth was three-and-a-half years older than
I, and whereas I felt at a disadvantage because I was not able
or allowed to do the things that she as an older child could

do, she must have had an even harder time, feeling that she was often being held back to the pace of a much younger sister. We scrapped a good deal, but I do not remember any protracted periods of anger. She and my brothers were really good to me, and although we've gone our separate ways, I have always felt a deep loyalty among us all.

Since I was not sent to school until I was almost six and had no friends my own age, I was lonely as a small child. I liked school very much; I enjoyed studying, athletics, and all the school activities. I made friends easily and never had any doubt that I was well liked. I was repeatedly elected president of my class, and later I was on the debating team and the basketball team and was editor of the school year-book. And yet I was not a happy child. I was tortured by neurotic symptoms: at first night terrors, then tics, a moth and butterfly phobia, compulsive "habits" and rituals. No one at that time had any understanding of these problems or of the suffering they could cause.

Another cause of my dissatisfaction, from perhaps eight or nine years of age, was a vague but disturbing feeling that all was not right with the world. Mollie and our house-keeper, Nellie, were always saying, "You're rich but we're poor people," and I knew from an early age that there must be a great difference between rich and poor. Sensing this made me feel uncomfortable. This feeling was reinforced by the sinking of the *Titanic* when I was ten. There was much excited talk among my relatives, who knew many of the passengers. I began to read the newspapers, and something— I don't know what—made me feel that people were con-cerned only about the rich (and their jewels) in this disaster.

Nellie often told us stories of the miserable voyage she and her family had taken from Ireland to the United States when she was a child. The poor traveled steerage, of course, and steerage in those days meant insufferable crowding, dirt, sickness, and hunger during the voyage. Steerage food was chiefly watery soup and potato peels. When in 1910—twenty or more years after Nellie's voyage—my family took me to

Europe, I looked down every day from our enclosed first-class deck to the open steerage deck below. Even in rainy or rough weather when the waves were pouring over the low, open space, crowds would gather there—men, women in their black shawls, and children of all ages. Many would gaze with pleading eyes at the first-class passengers above them, warm, dry, well fed, and luxuriously dressed. To this day, the very word "steerage" gives me a sick feeling.

By the time I was ten I was reading the books Nelson brought home from college. Two had a lasting influence on me: *Meditations of Marcus Aurelius* and Emerson's *Essays,* of which I remember best "Friendship" and "Self-Reliance." One textbook, *Everyday Ethics,* introduced many new thoughts to me and caused me to question much that I had taken for granted. At some point, perhaps in a discussion of wealth and poverty, the term *economics* was used, and I turned to Nelson's textook on economics but could not understand it. I'm not sure now whether it was *Everyday Ethics* or personal experiences that aroused my interest in women's rights. When I was eight, spending a summer with my family in England, I heard much talk about suffragettes and met two or three whom my parents knew. It was the first time I ever saw a woman smoke, and I remember wondering why it was more of a sin for a woman to smoke than for a man. I also thought it unfair that my brothers had always been given so much more freedom than my sister and I. I determined that if I ever had a daughter I would let her do everything a boy could do. At ten I organized and led a suffragette parade with my school friends.

When I was twelve the First World War broke out. I knew something about death, since my father, after a long illness at that time called Bright's Disease, had died the previous year at forty-six. Although I did not deeply grieve for him, I was impressed by the tragedy of early death and by my mother's suffering. The war really shook me; it seemed to make no sense at all. My family had always spoken well of the German people, and even after the United States entered

the war against Germany they were skeptical of the stories
of atrocities and the charge that all Germans were wicked.
Although I always had a strong feeling that I loved my country and was deeply concerned about Nelson, who joined the
army and was sent overseas, I was a pacifist from the beginning of the war, convinced that if I were a man of military
age I would refuse to fight. (It was not until the Spanish
Civil War in 1936 that I was to question my pacifism.)

From 1914 on I read the newspapers regularly and was
interested in discussions of world problems and current
events. I became more deeply involved when the Russian
Revolution occurred in March 1917. Although I was ap-
palled by the violence and bloodshed, the idea of a society
with a more nearly equal distribution of property, wealth,
and opportunity struck a responsive chord in me. There was
one person with whom I could openly and fearlessly talk as
I groped my way through these ideas: my history teacher,
Helen Boyce, an unusually well-educated and broad-minded
woman. She had a Ph.D. from the University of Chicago,
something quite unusual at that time for a woman teaching
in a girls' school. She had traveled widely and had taught
for some years at the American University of Beirut. Miss
Boyce never took for granted any set of values, and her aim
was always to teach her pupils to think, never to indoctri-
nate them. She was the first person with whom I felt really
free to discuss my unorthodox ideas, and she remained a
helpful and stimulating friend until her sudden, untimely
death when I was eighteen. Several of my brothers' friends,
to whom I had a strong, though usually one-sided, attachment, had died in their teens and twenties. These tragedies
caused me to work through my rather nebulous thoughts
about God and immortality, and before I was twenty I had
to recognize the fact that I could not believe in either con-
cept.

At school there were many girls I really liked and enjoyed;
we had great fun together and often interesting talks. And
yet with them I always felt, as I did with the members of

my family, a certain reserve. I could not talk with them about my inner feelings, about the things most important to me. This was not an intentional holding back, and indeed I was not altogether aware of it. Perhaps they weren't either.

My first close friend of about my age—just two years older— was my cousin Constance Morris, whom I had known all my life but began to know intimately when I was about twelve. Constance's family lived much of the time in Europe but traveled back and forth to the United States, and it was on one of these visits that they invited me to spend a week or so with them in a hotel outside Chicago. Constance and I shared a room, and the very first evening we talked most of the night. Constance had had experiences I had never dreamed of, living in many different countries, mostly with grown-ups who were leading fascinating and sophisticated lives—diplomats, royalty, artists, members of the theatrical world. Constance was a gifted, vivid story-teller with a great sense of humor and irony—talents I felt were lacking in my family, including myself. Hour after hour she enchanted me with her stories of the strange and exciting people she had known and her remarkable insights and forthright opinions. She did not hesitate to speak critically about her parents—something I would never have dared to do about mine.

At first I was the listener; then it became easy for me to talk too. Constance and Ira, her younger brother, were brought up by "Fräulein," their German governess, and an occasional tutor. They had seldom, if ever, gone to school. I believe Constance missed the companionship of girls her age; perhaps she also felt that I was her first real friend, in the same way that she was mine. "Let's not waste the night," Constance would say as soon as we were in bed and the lights were out, "we've got so much to talk about." She envied me my stable home and family, the summers at "Grey Rock," our big, hospitable country home on the shore of Green Lake, Wisconsin, and the relative simplicity of my life.

Constance's father, my uncle Ira, was United States Minister to Sweden, and on one of his trips to America during the first year or two of the First World War he tried to persuade my mother to let him take me back to Sweden as a companion for Constance. I don't know whether my mother would have let me go, even if I had wholeheartedly wanted to, but I myself was of two minds. It was very tempting to think of getting to know a new country and a new life, with Constance to show me the way; but I was a little frightened about crossing the ocean in wartime and also of having to learn a language of which I knew not a word. I was not sure how well I would get on with my uncle and aunt, both of whom, although bright, interesting, and amusing, were erratic and undependable. And I felt sure I would be homesick for Mollie. Mother made the decision: I would remain at home. How often have I wondered what my life would have been like had I gone! A few years later Constance came to the United States and was at Wellesley for several of the years I was there. She and her brother spent most of their vacations with us, something we all enjoyed.

My sister and I were brought up in a Victorian atmosphere of protection, and it was not until I went to college, just before I was seventeen, that I felt in any way free. My mother had gone for a year to Wellesley (class of 1892) but left when her older sister (who had been at Northwestern) died of tuberculosis; mother felt she should stay at home with my grandparents. It is interesting that although these two nineteenth-century girls went to college, of their seven brothers, older and younger, only the youngest did. He was Harold Swift, my favorite uncle, who remained all his life closely connected with the University of Chicago and was for a long time President of the Board of Trustees. My mother would have liked all her children to attend college, but Edward flatly refused. Before he had even finished high school, he wanted to work at the yards, as our father and all the Swift uncles did. Nelson went to Harvard for three years, but in spite of my mother's urging he would not return for his final year in the fall of 1913, when my father was dying. From then on Nelson also worked at the yards.

Ruth and I were given a choice of colleges: Wellesley, Smith, or Vassar. I would have liked a coeducational school, but the only one I knew anything about was the University of Chicago, and I wanted to be far away from home. There was no counseling available in those days, so I too chose Wellesley and entered in the fall of 1918, when Ruth was already a senior there.

Although Wellesley, founded by religious Protestants, had rather strict rules, I felt that the world had at last been opened to me. I could spend a whole day wandering alone in the woods or exploring Boston; I could have dinner with a boy without a chaperon. I didn't have to report or account to anyone, except that after 10 P.M. we were expected to be in our dormitories unless we received permission to stay out later in order to visit friends or spend a weekend in an "approved" inn. After the overprotection of home, this freedom—limited as it might seem today—was heaven.

Understandably, one of my most vivid and moving memories of my four years at Wellesley was of November 11, 1918. I was awakened just before dawn by the tolling of the bells of all the churches. Running to the open window, I could discern a few figures in the still-dark streets. "Peace has come," they shouted, "the war is over, God be praised." I dressed and went out just as the eastern sky showed streaks of red and orange heralding the sunrise of the first day of peace after more than four years of war. I had a moment's thought of going into a church, any church, to share in the thanksgiving. But instead I chose to walk alone along the wooded banks of the Charles River.

The armistice did not lessen my interest in what was happening in the world. I read the *Christian Science Monitor* daily, followed with excitement the momentous changes taking place in European governments, the dissolution of the Austro-Hungarian empire, the establishment of new countries, the growth of anticolonialism, the earthshaking but obscure events in Russia. I could not help being aware of the terrible suffering and hunger in much of the world, and occasionally direct appeals came to Wellesley from colleges, schools, or individuals in Europe. For a year or two I was chairman of a committee formed to deal with these touching, often heartbreaking, appeals, some of which we were able to meet from a college fund established for the purpose. One letter was from the University of Vienna, asking our help for their sick or starving students. The committee members all agreed to send them as much as we fairly could.

Another letter, which did not seem to fit in exactly with the committee goals, I dealt with personally. It was addressed to a Wellesley professor who had died a few years earlier and was written by a woman in southern Germany who had apparently become rather well acquainted with this teacher during a long train trip in Europe. Now this Bavarian woman wrote about her three small children who literally were starving in these terrible postwar years and begged for help. I think I must have sent her money (I don't remember whether it was possible to send food at that time) and a personal letter. Possibly I did so more than once. I remember—and mention—this incident because of an interesting sequel. About 1946, when I was living in Pennington, New Jersey, I received in an envelope from Wellesley College a letter from southern Germany addressed to Helen Muriel Morris (my maiden name) at the college dormitory where I had lived twenty-five years earlier. It was from this same Bavarian woman, not unlike the first letter except that now, after World War II, she had not only children but also grandchildren suffering from hunger. She enclosed, as proof of authenticity, I suppose, the envelope of one of the letters I had written to her years earlier, with my name printed in the corner and addressed to her in handwriting which I recognized as my own but which now seemed to me surprisingly childlike in its careful, rigid lines. This time I was able to send food packages directly—much more valuable than money in this second period of appalling scarcity of food in central Europe.

Possibly these letters, especially the one from the University of Vienna, had something to do with an incident I find a little embarrassing to relate. I did not like living in luxury when so many people—and perhaps I was thinking particularly of European students—had not even the barest necessities. These troubling thoughts formed themselves into a phrase in my mind, namely, that I wanted to become "independent of material things." I never thought of trying to starve myself or of giving up my education or my future plans to travel, but I became more and more inclined to do away with what I considered luxuries. It was not hard to give my friends the clothes I liked best, including my fur coat and my jewelry. (I kept the string of pearls that my father, dying, had left to be given me on my thirteenth birthday, and I kept a necklace of semiprecious stones belonging to my mother, which I had loved as a child and which she gave me on my sixteenth birthday. It seemed right to me, in gratitude to my parents, to keep these two gifts, which I still have.)

But one thing was hard to do. Since the age of eleven or twelve I had been a book collector and I had a number of interesting first or early editions of books I cared about, and a few with very beautiful leather bindings. An ascetic streak in me made me think for a while that I ought to burn them if I was really to make myself "independent." At the same time, the beauty-loving side of my nature rebelled at destroying anything so beautiful and so worthy of love. Part of me recognized what I have called my asceticism as a form of pride and selfishness. Finally, after long doubts and struggles, I found a solution which I have never regretted: I would sell my beloved books and send the money to the Austrian students. Not with a heavy heart, but with a feeling of embarrassment which I could not dispel, I carried a big suitcase of books into the Boston bookshop where I had purchased a few of these treasures and told the manager I wanted to sell them. It seemed to me that he must think me the strangest creature in the world, but he was so polite and matter-of-fact that I got through the ordeal better than I had expected I would, and when I sent the money off to Austria I felt I had chosen the right solution.

I succeeded in accomplishing my goal of caring very little about material possessions. In general, I liked reading in a library or borrowing library books quite as well as owning them and preferred seeing great pictures in a museum to having them on my walls. For years, personal comfort meant very little to me, though it is becoming more important as time goes on. For a long time I felt guilty and distressed about spending money on myself, but the fact that most of my extravagances gave pleasure to my friends soothed my guilt somewhat. For instance, the little weekend cottage I had in the Vienna Woods, referred to frequently in these pages, was indeed a joy to me, my daughter, and our friends, as it continues to be. It provided for many friends and acquaintances a vacation they could not otherwise have had and later served as a refuge. As I grow older, I am increasingly thankful for my independent income. Although I am grateful every day of my life for the food I eat and other essentials, I am also glad to have experienced hunger for some months in Paris in 1945, living on French rations before and after the end of the Second World War.

At college, though I believe I always had one, I did not wear a watch for two years (also with the aim of becoming independent) and succeeded in developing such an accurate bodily or mental clock that I almost always know the time, even when I wake in the night. Probably this required just a little training of a natural tendency which some people have and others do not. In earlier years in Chicago, I used to enjoy disciplining myself by taking cold showers in winter or sleeping on the floor. Yet I have always had a great love of beauty and of pleasure and in some cases even of profusion and excess. How can one explain these contradictions? Perhaps by my two sets of genes—those of the Morrises, some of whom were erratic, extravagant, flagrant, tending toward excess, and those of the Swifts, moderate, reasonable, cool? The older I grow, the more I feel myself at heart a Morris, though the Swift moderation has usually been in control. But even this attempt at an explanation is too simple.

At Wellesley I had several teachers whom I liked and truly admired. My philosophy teacher, Mary Whiton Calkins, was outstanding, not only for her brilliant mind and scholarship, but most of all for her intellectual integrity. Although we were not friends in a personal sense, she had a great influence on my thinking. Two other teachers and several girls at college became my lifelong friends. In my junior year at Wellesley I became well acquainted with two fellow students, Kay Cooke and Betty Sanford, both of whom had considerable influence on my development. Kay was much more outgoing than I, and she persuaded me to see more people and do more things. It may have been Kay who got me to try out for the debating team, and in this way I came to know Betty, who was also on the team. Kay was, I think, my first contemporary who criticized me in a friendly or humorous way, which did me a lot of good.

It was at this time that I joined a new organization, called the Wellesley Forum, set up to discuss political questions and current events. That same year, through John Rothschild, a friend at Harvard, I got together with a group of about six Harvard and Radcliffe students, and we organized an intercollegiate conference with a view to forming a nationwide body of students with liberal leanings, interested in national and world problems. A few hundred students from many colleges gathered at Harvard during spring vacation in 1921 for this conference, to which we had invited well-known speakers, mostly liberals and Socialists. I had been appointed "toastmistress" to introduce the speakers. After the speeches and discussions, representatives from each college met with our organizing group to work out a constitution and to elect officers. This organization, first called the Intercollegiate Liberal League, later became the National Student Forum. I was elected president for the coming year. During my term I attended a number of conferences or weekend camps of already existing organizations, mostly Socialist or social democratic, although some were run by liberal religious groups such as the Quakers and the Fellowship of Reconciliation. In this way I became acquainted with many interesting and prominent people, including Norman Thomas and Roger Baldwin, both of whom I was able to persuade to speak at the Wellesley Forum, of which I became president the next year. I looked up to these "old men" (both were in their late thirties) with awe. Later I voted twice for Norman Thomas, Socialist candidate for president of the United States, and was present at his eightieth birthday celebration. Roger Baldwin, "Founder of the American Civil Liberties Union," with whom I maintained close contact since 1940, remained an alert and energetic man until shortly before his death, on August 26, 1981, at age ninety-seven.

The summer of 1921, between my junior and senior years, I spent in England. My sister and I did something rather unusual for girls at that time, unusual at least in England: we hiked ("took a walking trip," it was called) through the Cotswolds, North Wales, and the Lake District, all of which we enjoyed in spite of the frequent rain. In the Lake District I collected flowers mentioned by Wordsworth, pressed them, and made a little booklet with one flower and the appropriate quotation on each page. There I also had the delightful experience of bathing nude under a waterfall for the first time. One week we spent in London, where I met and talked with several noted Englishmen who took an interest in our intercollegiate student organization. Among them I became acquainted with the political scientist Harold Laski, who had already lectured at Harvard and Yale and later became chairman of the British Labour party.

Back in the United States, I soon found I had acquired a

reputation of being a "Red" or a "Bolshie," as anyone left of center was called in those days. I think this was particularly because of my attending the Sacco-Vanzetti trial, which took place in Dedham, not far from Wellesley, and taking a strong stand on their side. Calvin Coolidge, then vice-president, wrote a series of three articles called "Enemies of the Republic," published in the popular magazine *The Delineator*. In the first of these articles, "Are the 'Reds' Stalking Our College Women?," I fancied I detected references to myself. Coolidge wrote bitterly against Socialists, some of whom I knew, and attacked two of the wisest and most admired Wellesley professors, Vida D. Scudder and Mary Whiton Calkins.*

I should perhaps mention one incident which occurred, I think, in my senior year. We had of course a student government, to which I paid little attention, since it seemed to me a wishy-washy affair. There had always been, while I was in college, an "honor system," which meant simply that each girl was "on her honor" to put a slip in a designated box if she was going to be out after 10 P.M., stating at which of the previously approved places she would be and the date and time she expected to return to the dormitory. I don't know quite how it happened that this was suddenly changed (or perhaps there was simply word that it was about to be changed?) to a system whereby one would be obliged to report on one's neighbor if one knew that she was lying or cheating. This aroused considerable indignation among many of us, and I got together with a half-dozen or more girls to decide what we could do about it. I believe it was my idea—my thoughts often being deep in European history—to follow Martin Luther's example and post theses on the chapel door. Several of us composed and signed our theses

*Calvin Coolidge, "Are the 'Reds' Stalking Our College Women?," *The Delineator* (New York), vol. 98, no. 5, June 1921. (This is one of three articles under the general heading "Enemies of the Republic.")

and early one morning posted them, with blank pages for other supporting signatures, on the doors of the Wellesley chapel. This caused an enormous sensation; masses of signatures were added, including many by faculty members, who also congratulated the composers of the theses. Discussions sprang up all over; it became clear that most people were against the new "dishonor system," and it was promptly abolished.

It may have been this incident, along with my being president of the Forum, and perhaps the fact that I was known as a pacifist, that caused me to be the student selected to speak on disarmament at a large Wellesley meeting in 1922, to which many Wellesley alumnae and trustees and faculty from several other colleges had been invited. (A disarmament conference, to which the United States had issued invitations to a number of foreign governments, was at that time in progress in Washington.) Although I easily took part in or led discussions, I hated making public speeches and was afraid to accept. I believe it was chiefly Kay Cooke who persuaded me to do so. I know that when I told Kay I intended to leave what I would say to the inspiration of the moment, she replied vigorously that I had to think it out and write it out ahead of time. I didn't write it out, but I did give it much thought, again walking along the Charles River, and I made a few notes. How grateful I was for Kay's insistence when it turned out—I don't know how or why— to be a tremendously well-received speech. I had thought of it as something extremely simple. Perhaps it was the simplicity which appealed to people tired of complicated and wordy talk. I received any number of appreciative letters from strangers as well as from Wellesley faculty members and many invitations to speak at various meetings and clubs. There was even a request for me to talk at Carnegie Hall, which nothing in the world would have persuaded me to accept.

In our last months at college Kay proposed that we make an effort to know some of the more interesting students, mostly in classes below ours, with whom we had had little contact, and a few of the teachers we did not know. We had a series of meetings, sometimes with one, sometimes with two or more new acquaintances; but the most interesting occurred toward the end of our senior year, when we were so busy with examinations, final papers, and all the paraphernalia of preparing to graduate that our only free time was from six to eight in the morning. We asked Betty Sanford, Gladys Lack, Margaret Willard, and a girl I shall call Andrea (because of her involvement in political problems later, she would not wish me to use her real name) to a picnic breakfast with us on a grassy, violet-dappled hill one May morning. Our breakfast of bread and milk and strawberries was simple, but the excitement of conversation made up for any lack of grandeur. I clearly remember our discussion originating from a remark by Margaret, a girl born in Bulgaria of a Greek woman whose husband had deserted her and their two young children. The mother, with Margaret, then four or five years old, and a son of about seven, was adopted by a New England Protestant missionary who brought the family to America. Margaret's mother died a year or so later, and Margaret was raised by this missionary, whom she called "Grandmother" and who was the elderly widow of a Civil War veteran. When she developed a long physical and mental illness during Margaret's adolescence, Margaret interrupted her high school studies and took complete care of her grandmother until her death some years later. Margaret then returned to high school, where a teacher, discerning her unusual intellectual qualities and her appreciation of the arts, encouraged and helped her to work toward going to college. When Margaret entered Wellesley, a year after I did, she was seven years older than I, but I never felt the difference in our ages. In spite of her difficult life, the depths of her emotions, and her seriousness, she could be joyful, lighthearted, and witty. Margaret's strong religious feelings had drawn her to the Anglo-Catholic Church, I suppose because, in the largely Protestant community in which she had grown up, it was the religion she encountered most closely resembling the Greek Orthodox Church of her early childhood. She had recently become an Anglo-Catholic.

The remark that kindled our lively discussion related to some church holy day, in reference to which Margaret spoke with complete conviction of Christ rising from the tomb. "I don't believe in that," said Betty quietly. "Oh, I do, I do," exclaimed Margaret—and suddenly we were all expressing our religious beliefs or lack of them. This was the first of many breakfasts on "the Hill," as we always called it, and though I got to know these girls well only in the last month of college, they are the ones who remained my closest friends. I saw every one of them at some time during my years in Europe, and later more often in America. (Only Kay and I, Kay who did so much for me and of whom I have such happy memories, have drifted apart. I don't know why.)

Since, along with Constance Morris, these girls were the earliest of my lifelong friends, I must say a little more about them. Betty had a gentle voice and a serene face, which led one to believe she had a mind at peace with the world. Actually, she was grappling hard with political and world problems. I believe Betty had the keenest intellect of us all. Impatient to finish college in order to go on to graduate study and work as an economist, she completed her last two years of college in one—a hitherto unheard-of feat at Wellesley—and graduated in 1922, Phi Beta Kappa. Betty generously credited me with giving her the incentive and confidence to undertake this task (just as, a few years later, Margaret thanked me—an atheist— for giving her the courage to become a Roman Catholic when I realized how sincerely she desired it). In spite of Betty's sharpness of mind and ardent determination to work for a better world, her gentle manner was a true expression of her character as I knew her then—with her love of nature and animals, of fantasy and happy fairy tales—and later—as with gentle, loving strength she brought up her three children.

Andrea, a tall, blond girl from the Midwest, was also involved in politics, economics, world problems. After college, in the 1920s, I saw Andrea at such times as we were both in New York. Gladys, who remained a close friend to us both, was often with us. I saw Andrea again in 1932, on my first visit to the Soviet Union. She was studying in Moscow, where I spent three weeks that August. I am not sure when she returned to the United States, but since I remained in Europe until 1939 there were many years when we were out of touch. We next had the opportunity to meet in New York at a conference that Andrea, now working in some administrative position in a hospital, attended. Andrea had married an American, Jim, an older man of great personal charm who wrote good children's stories under several pseudonyms. We liked each other immediately. Both Andrea and Jim, idealistic left-of-center thinkers, were suspect in the United States and had their share of being persecuted here as "unAmerican." Whenever there was a possibility to get together, we would do so, sometimes with Glad also. These meetings were arranged with all due caution. Jim died in the late 1970s, and Andrea about two years after Jim.

Gladys, born in England, was eight years old when her family immigrated to the United States. Her schooling, like Margaret's, was interrupted by the necessity to work. From age fourteen she helped support the family by taking on typing and secretarial jobs. In her second job at the YWCA in New York she, like Margaret, met an older woman in a superior position who recognized her gifts and urged her to complete her studies and prepare for college by going to night school. Her mentor, again like Margaret's, was a Wellesley graduate, and Gladys after one year at a state university in New York entered Wellesley. Gladys was four years older than I, but a year behind me in college. However, in one of my last years, we were both enrolled in an elective course in history and one in writing. I was impressed, as Glad's friends at the YWCA must have been, by her talent in writing and her sensitive perception and understanding of human beings. From our first meeting on "the Hill" I realized what a difficult childhood and early youth Gladys had had, yet in a way I was a little envious of her experience of hard work and sacrifice. These had given her a sense of being useful and a broader knowledge of "everyday life" than I had ever had. I could not rid myself of a feeling of guilt because of my privileged situation.

After college Margaret, Glad, and I were often together in Europe and America. We were a wonderfully congenial trio, nicknamed by a Viennese friend "the Cloverleaf." When we traveled together we loved to observe people on shipboard, in trains, or in hotels or pensions, sometimes even in restaurants or at a concert, and would give them names and try to imagine their lives. Or we would each offer a name of a character and write a short story with the three characters in the principal roles; then each of us read her story aloud to the other two. When we saw something that aroused our interest or wonder, such as a little city on an Italian hilltop, we might each write a poem about it.

Margaret and I, the winter we were both in Vienna, named the people we would observe in concerts: there were "the Fair Girl," "the Brown-velvet-jacket Man," "Blackbeard," and many others. "Blackbeard" turned out to be Mark Brunswick, who later married my analyst, Dr. Ruth Mack. And one concert-goer—I think we called him "Jeremy"— was, I learned, the father of Freud's "Little Hans."

Margaret and Gladys both became teachers in excellent private schools for girls. After some years Margaret retired, married, and lived with her husband in Grandmother's house in Madison, Connecticut. She was often occupied in caring for her brother's three daughters while their mother was away. Margaret led a busy but relatively quiet life, dedicated to helping others and being active in town meetings and the church. Not only for her own household but also for her friends she sewed, cooked, preserved the garden fruits and vegetables. Everything she made, even an apron or a jar of raspberry jam, was a small work of art. She designed and made beautiful hooked rugs; laid out and tended an exquisite garden. One felt that everything Margaret undertook was accomplished with love. Margaret died in 1964, less than a year after the death of my cousin, Constance Morris.

Gladys, early in the Depression, became dissatisfied with teaching in a school isolated from the vast number of troubled, jobless young people of the 1930s. She got work at the National Youth Administration, where she had on-the-job training in vocational counseling, and worked there for some years and at other counseling offices, including a stint at the Veteran's Hospital connected with the Menninger Clinic. After several months there, however, word came from Washington that the counselor must himself be a veteran.

Gladys returned to New York. She had earlier been psychoanalyzed, and one of her analyst friends referred her to the Carolyn Zachary Institute, which needed the services of teachers who had been analyzed. The board of directors of this institute included a number of distinguished psychoanalysts, among them Berta Bornstein, Grace Abbate, and Marianne Kris. After some years of work there with children with learning difficulties, Gladys was referred to the Child Study Center at Yale University, where Ernst Kris was organizing a pilot study of infancy. For eight years Glad was employed on the team as an observer of infants and nursery-school children, at the same time continuing the type of work she had done in New York as a tutor in her home.

In 1959 Glad moved to Washington, where she devoted herself again to remedial education. She has since retired but continues to work part-time in her home and as a consultant in schools. Betty, too, lives in Washington, and on my occasional visits there I love to see both these friends.

Of the men I knew in my college days, the only one who remained my friend all his life was Brooks Phillips. I met him at the Middlebury Summer School of English at Breadloaf, Vermont, when I was eighteen. I at first mistook him for my contemporary but soon learned that he was doing graduate work and teaching at Harvard and was ten years older than I. Brooks and I took long walks together almost every afternoon that summer, talking about writing and literature and philosophy and about ourselves. In later years we wrote to each other frequently. Several times we were able to visit together for a few days or a week although we lived far apart. Brooks died suddenly at the age of fifty. His two sons I seldom see but am very attached to.

I have moved far ahead of the chronological story of my pre-Vienna years, but these early friends have been of such significance throughout my life—each one influencing my personality, my thinking, and my work—that in a sense they are truly a part of me.

I graduated from Wellesley in 1922, with a bachelor of arts degree, having majored in literature and history. From an early age I had wanted to be a teacher, although my mother tried to discourage me, feeling—with justification at that time—that a woman teacher's life was likely to be very limited. But college intensified my interest in education and my desire to work in that field. Before settling down to graduate work, however, I wanted a year in Italy—my dream for many years—and this seemed the right time. I sailed for Italy in September 1922 with Kay. Partly because I knew my mother would be more willing to let me go to Europe if I were connected with some school, I had applied to the American School of Classical Studies in Rome (I had taken courses in Latin, Roman history, and archaeology at college) and was, as I wished, accepted on a flexible basis. I attended the school irregularly, chiefly to use the library, go on school-sponsored expeditions, and take part in parties and entertainments. We lived in Rome with a fascinating Italian family, from whom I learned not only the language but a great deal about people and life in a culture completely different from any I had known. This year was in every respect, except the formal one, an education.

The next two years I spent at Oxford, doing graduate work

in English literature as a preparation for teaching. I had spent some days in Oxford after my junior year at college and had fallen in love with the beautiful town. When I decided to begin graduate work in Europe, Oxford was my choice.

During the three long vacations every year I usually traveled to the continent. One summer Betty and I took a trip on a cargo boat up the Norwegian coast, to North Cape and back, stopping a few hours daily at the coastal villages or towns. Another time Gladys, who was in Oxford during my second year there, and I spent six weeks in Greece, where we traveled around the Peloponnesus mostly on mule-back—the only means of locomotion except foot. Following that we were snowbound for a week in Delphi's one small hotel. One summer I invited Mollie and Nellie to spend a few weeks with me in Ireland. I returned several times to my beloved Rome and Sicily and in 1925 spent a week in Berlin, my first visit to Germany.

I found Oxford rather bleak, rigid, and unfriendly to women students. After Wellesley, and especially after my year of complete freedom in Italy, I felt as penned in as if I were in a girls' boarding school. I remember being "ticked off"—as the British would say—by the college principal for "being seen walking on the street without a hat." Another time, on vacation in Italy, Kathleen Theobald, the only English friend I made at Oxford, and I decided to stretch the vacation out to Monday morning instead of returning to Oxford on Sunday as we were supposed to do. It happened that there was a frightful wreck on the train we ought to have taken the previous day, killing about two hundred passengers. We thanked our lucky stars that we had delayed. When the principal called us to her office to reprimand us, Kathleen commented that, in view of the wreck, we were lucky to be there at all. "That is beside the point, Miss Theobald," was the principal's reply.

After two years at Oxford I worked half a year at the British Museum to complete my thesis, a life of Mary Shelley. I did not at the time examine my reasons for choosing this

subject, but I now see a significance in the fact that Mary
was the daughter of the leftist, nonconformist political phi-
losopher William Godwin and of Mary Wollstonecraft, the
courageous sponsor of women's rights. Mary Shelley was
not only the wife of an idealistic, radical poet and a gifted,
imaginative author in her own right—the creator of Fran-
kenstein and his monster—but also a fearless, independent
young woman who defied convention and conformity in
joining her life to Shelley's. My obtaining a degree at Oxford
depended entirely on my thesis and an oral examination
regarding my thesis by three Oxford dons, two of them cler-
gymen and the third a woman of obviously rigid mind. The
questions were exclusively about my moral and religious
attitudes as expressed or not expressed in my thesis. I was
told, for instance, "You have nowhere stated that you condemn suicide."

"Because I *don't* condemn it," I replied. "And besides I
think such a remark would be out of place here."

"But surely you know suicide is a sin," said the woman
examiner. It was not clear whether this was a statement or
a question, and I did not reply. The ordeal continued in this
vein, and I left feeling fairly certain that I had failed. Two
weeks later I received a notice to that effect. When I then
wrote to my examiners asking for their criticisms of the
scholarship or style of my thesis and suggesting that I might
improve it and submit it again, they replied that they did
not think it would be useful to do so. Obviously the matter
was closed.

Friends have wondered why I was not depressed. I was
angry for a short while, but my predominant feeling was
that the situation was too ridiculous to be taken seriously.
I had always done well in literature and in writing and had
no doubt that I could get a Ph.D. in America relatively easily. Several years later I submitted three sections of this
rejected thesis as separate essays to the London *Mercury*,
one of the best English literary magazines at that time. They
were accepted, and the first one was immediately published.

To my disappointment the magazine went bankrupt or changed management, so the two remaining papers were never published, nor did I ever receive payment for any of them. I had looked forward to the promised sum as the first money earned by my writing.

I shall pass over most of the events and my emotions of the 1920s and early 1930s, except those which have a direct bearing on my life after 1934. In the spring of 1926 I decided to go to Vienna to explore the possibility of being psychoanalyzed by Freud. I was persuaded to take this step less by inner conviction than by what I might call external pressures when I was in a difficult personal situation. The only analysts whose names I knew were Freud, Jung, and Adler, and I knew very little about psychoanalysis. I had met a few young American doctors who had spent part of a year in Vienna doing medical work, some of whom had had a few months of analysis, but what they told me made very little sense to me. At Wellesley I had read but one psychoanalytic book—*The Freudian Wish*, by Edwin B. Holt—which I had picked up by chance while roaming in the stacks of the college library. I really did not understand it too well; nevertheless, this book must have left some sort of positive impression on me and certainly aroused my curiosity.

Arriving in Vienna one May afternoon, when the streets and parks were filled with the scent of lilac, I immediately sat down and wrote a letter to Freud asking whether he would accept me as a patient. I promptly received a brief, polite reply indicating his regret that he was unable to take me but referring me to his pupil and colleague Dr. Ruth Mack (after her marriage, Dr. Brunswick). I copied Dr. Mack's address and telephone number in my address book, tore up Freud's letter, and dropped it in the wastebasket. (I am sure the Freud Archives will never forgive this act of vandalism!) Dr. Mack, who was living in Vienna, was an American, the daughter of Judge Julian Mack, with whose name I was familiar since he had been a highly respected judge in the Chicago Juvenile Court, the first juvenile court in the world.

Although I was disappointed that Freud had not accepted me, I was at the same time relieved to have an analyst whose native language was English and who had gone to school, college, and medical school in the United States.

I had several consultations with Dr. Mack in which I told her my problems and reasons for considering analysis, not omitting my doubts and questions. I remember telling her I had heard that analysis might take six months and possibly even eight or nine. She replied matter-of-factly that it might take several years. Although this was rather a shock, everything she said made such good sense and seemed so down-to-earth that I decided to be analyzed. I felt some trepidation, but knew myself well enough to feel pretty sure that, if I were to begin analysis, I would go through with it, come hell or high water.

Dr. Mack told me she was going to the United States to spend the summer with her father in New York and gave me the choice of beginning analysis in New York in late June or starting in Vienna in September. It was not unusual at that time for analysts to take long summer vacations and to suggest to one or more patients who were free to move about and wanted to get ahead as quickly as possible that they accompany them to the vacation spot. I was eager to begin; besides, I had intended to pay a brief visit to my mother in Green Lake, and I liked the idea of two months in New York, where several of my Wellesley friends were living. So it happened that, because of my analyst's personal plans, I spent the summers of both 1926 and 1927 in New York. I had an analytic hour six days a week, attended some summer courses at Columbia, and became involved in an interesting and, to me, new sort of social life. Betty Sanford was doing graduate work in economics at Columbia and brought me together with a number of her friends and acquaintances, mostly leftist intellectuals ten or twenty years older than we were, who, however, had the gift of making us feel their equals. They were teachers, lawyers and judges, consultants to labor unions, or persons engaged with the unions in some other capacity. There was an attitude of general camaraderie among us all, men and women. Many of the married couples seemed rather independent of each other, wives and husbands often dating someone of the opposite sex in accord with the mores of the "roaring twenties." In groups or in couples, we would go to speakeasies during those Prohibition evenings or give a party or picnic if we had got hold of some tolerable drinks. But these lively evenings or weekends were not just a new kind of fun for me; they were always interesting and stimulating because the people were essentially serious, full of ideas and ideals, and enthusiastic about their work. Many of these people were already well known. They included Walter W. Stewart, a political economist whom I liked particularly and who later became a faculty member and for a time acting president of the Institute for Advanced Studies at Princeton; the labor leaders Sidney Hillman and Morris Hillquit; and Judge Learned Hand. We all called each other by our first names, except that I could never bring myself to call Judge Hand "Learned."

Most of the time I lived in Greenwich Village, where I made some new acquaintances, among them—again through Betty—the celebrated Russian sculptor Sergei Konenkov and his beautiful, gracious wife, Margarita, adored by everyone who knew her, who soon became, and has remained, one of my dearest friends. (This apolitical sculptor, devoted to art and, like all Russians I have known, to his country, was invited back to Russia as "Sculptor of the Russian People" in 1945, and I was able to visit the Konenkovs in Moscow several times after that.)

I found the Village a delightful place to live, Bohemian of course, truly villagelike in the friendliness of neighbors and strangers, amusing, accepting of nonconformists and eccentrics. It did not bother me that my tiny top-floor apartment, sublet from Kay, was so unbearably hot that I often slept on the roof, no matter how dirty, or spent many nights riding an open double-decker bus or the Staten Island ferry, each costing, I believe, five cents.

I returned with my analyst to Austria in September 1926 and began to get acquainted with the city of Vienna. Although Austria was still poor, it was beginning to recover from the horrors and hardships of the First World War. After receiving some relief from the United States and Great Britain, Austria had, in late 1922, obtained a large loan through the League of Nations, enabling it to put an end to the frightful inflation. (Nevertheless, to my complete bewilderment, many people still gave the price of everyday objects, such as bread or a pair of shoes, as costing so and so many thousands of schillings.)

With the dissolution of the Hapsburg Empire at the end of the war, Austria had been reduced to a small, mostly German-speaking country. There were two strong political parties: the Christian Social party (always called the Christian Socialists though they had nothing to do with socialism), made up largely of Catholic peasants and of conservative landowners, army officers, and big businessmen; and the Social Democrats, often called simply Socialists, chiefly working class, with strong intellectual leaders, including Otto Bauer and Friedrich Adler. The Social Democrats were strongest in Vienna, where about a third of the entire Austrian population lived, whereas the Christian Socialists had a majority in the country. A few brief Communist attempts at a putsch in 1919 were easily put down by the other parties, for the Socialists were as determined as the conservatives to resist Communist agitation.

There was a tendency in the provinces to break away from Vienna—partly for ideological reasons, but principally because they resented sending food supplies to the city in the postwar years of shortages and hardship. The Social Democrats were obliged to make some concessions to the provinces; in return Vienna was elevated to the rank of a state, and the mayor of Vienna became the equivalent of a state governor. Socialist-controlled Vienna—"Red Vienna" it was often called—pursued autonomous policies and put great emphasis on working-class housing, adult education, and health, under the leadership of three or four unusually able men. One of these leaders, Julius Tandler, later my professor of anatomy at the university, was known throughout Vienna for his brilliant lectures and even more for his mordant wit. Vienna was at that time a uniquely progressive city. I visited new workers' apartments and a number of very interesting schools for children and for adults. I was impressed by the absence of slums, the clean streets, the well-tended parks, and the beautiful Wiener Wald—the Vienna Woods. I was enthusiastic about the success of obligatory health insurance, something most Americans then considered absolutely immoral.

Margaret, my friend from "the Hill" at Wellesley, was in Vienna that year, and I had a Christmas visit from Kathleen, my Oxford friend. Otherwise it would have been a rather lonely year, since I did not really make friends with anyone. I loved the Wiener Wald, through which I would wander with Trojan, my German shepherd; and Margaret and I reveled in Vienna's marvelous music, attending a concert or an opera four or five times a week. (It was the Beethoven year.) We bought a record player and some classical records and played them over until we knew them by heart. I found a good teacher and took piano lessons. Margaret and I, who both had had a smattering of Greek in college, struggled together through the *Odyssey* in Greek. I worked two or three afternoons a week as apprentice to a bookbinder. On the whole, it was a good year.

I was, of course, deeply involved in my analysis, as anyone who takes it seriously is bound to be. During this first period of my analysis, which lasted three years, I was always looking forward to the end and was more than once tempted to give it up. For one thing, I chafed at being so much confined to Vienna when all of Europe was, so to speak, at my doorstep. During this period I had only one long vacation, and I used it for traveling, mostly in out-of-the-way places in western Europe, exploring small towns, little villages, and the countryside, sometimes sleeping in the woods under a blanket, sleeping bags being still unknown to me.

I always had great respect for Dr. Brunswick. She handled my analysis skillfully, though I must have been a difficult patient. I am not unmindful of her occasional mistakes (is there any analyst who does not make mistakes?), but she was fair and willing to admit her errors. The one characteristic to which I really objected was that she tried, I think, to control or influence my way of life too much, as many analysts did in the 1920s. I particularly admired Dr. Brunswick's feeling for essentials, her swift penetration to the heart of the matter. Although not regarded so at that time, she was what we would now consider very young. She was twenty-eight when I began my analysis, having already been in practice for about four years. I never found her youth a disadvantage.

Many features of analysis at that time would now be disapproved of in the United States: analysts stated their opinions and tastes more openly and often discussed them freely with patients; some analysts were less stringent than we are now in avoiding social contact with patients; many did not object to their patients' knowing each other, and some even suggested their making contact if one was likely to be able to be of help to another. For example, it was through Dr. Brunswick that I first met "the Wolf-Man" (the Russian-born subject of Freud's *From the History of an Infantile Neurosis*) when I wanted to study Russian; she knew he would be glad to have extra work. Another of her patients, the subject of her "Analysis of a Case of Paranoia (Delusions of Jealousy)," occasionally did some sewing and alterations for me, though I never became well acquainted with her. Dr. Brunswick sometimes told me that she had talked over some problem of mine with "the Professor"—as she always called Freud—and would quote his opinion. Whether this was good technique or not, I admit it pleased me. Though I cannot generalize about other analysts of that time, some of their patients have told me of similar experiences. (Possibly this tendency, even if infrequent, may have given the Wolf-Man some realistic ground to believe that Dr. Brunswick discussed his case with Freud.)*

I think I asked only one "favor" of Dr. Brunswick during my entire analysis—that she introduce me to Professor Freud—but I was very insistent about it. I was happy when she later complied, saying, "The Freuds have asked me to bring you to tea at their home next Sunday afternoon." I am not sure in which year this meeting took place. Since I was not in Vienna during any of the midsummers of this period, it must have been in early or late summer, for the visit took place not in the Berggasse but in a house the Freuds had taken for the summer in a Vienna suburb, perhaps Grinzing or Heiligenstadt. It was a family gathering except for Dr. Brunswick and myself, on a sunny afternoon when it was pleasant to sit on the veranda or wander around the garden. Frau Professor was of course hostess, but several other family members were present, including "Tante Minna." I have an impression also of Freud's mother but cannot be sure whether I really met her or see her only in my mind's eye

*Freud's *From the History of an Infantile Neurosis* (1918 [1914]) can be found in the *Standard Edition*, vol. 17 (London: Hogarth Press Limited, 1955), Dr. Brunswick's article in *Journal of Nervous and Mental Disease* 70 (1929):1–22, 155–78. Brunswick mentions the Wolf-Man's suspicions regarding her discussing his case with Freud in "A Supplement to Freud's 'History of an Infantile Neurosis,' " *International Journal of Psycho-Analysis* 9 (1928):439, reprinted in *The Psychoanalytic Reader*, ed. Robert Fliess, M.D. (New York: International Universities Press, Inc., 1948). "He added that through me he was really getting all the benefit of Freud's knowledge and experience, without coming directly under his influence. When I asked how this was possible, he said that he was sure I discussed all the details of his case with Freud, so as to be advised by him! I remarked that this was not the case . . ." [Fleiss, *Psychoanalytic Reader*, p. 84].

from Dr. Brunswick's vivid description. Naturally I was prepared to be impressed by Freud, and I was impressed, more
by his face, his expressive penetrating eyes, and his earnest
but charming manner than by anything he said. A serious
discussion would not have been appropriate, nor would I
have been able to overcome my shyness enough to take part
in one. This simple family afternoon, filled with friendliness
and hospitality, culminated in a magnificent *Jause*, the Austrian equivalent of the English "high tea." I was happy and
grateful to have had this experience.

I must return to the summer of 1927, which I had spent
continuing my analysis in New York, to mention two political events that affected me strongly and made me very
sad. One was the execution of Sacco and Vanzetti. The other
was trouble in Austria between the Christian Socialists, with
their reactionary Heimwehr ("Home Defense Forces," a sort
of legal private army), and the Social Democrats, with their
own armed force, the Schutzbund or "Defense League." In
July 1927, in a clash between them, a child and an old man
were shot, apparently accidentally, by the reactionary forces.
When the Heimwehr members who alledgedly fired the shots
were acquitted by a Vienna jury, the Social Democrats called
for a mass demonstration. Street fighting broke out between
the police, controlled by the Christian Socialists, who formed
the majority of the Austrian government, and the demon-
strators, during which almost one hundred persons were killed
and the Ministry of Justice was burned down. The Christian
Socialist government used this opportunity for a violent assertion of authority, a turning point in the balance of Socialist and non-Socialist forces. Reading the reports in the
New York papers about this tragic incident, I literally shiv-
ered for the future. Though this was certainly not the beginning of political dissension in Austria, it was the beginning
of my understanding of it and of my deeper concern for the
fate of the country itself.

I became more interested in Germany also. I had now and

then spent a few days in Germany since first settling in
Austria in 1926. I had seen ill-clothed, unemployed men,
singly or in pairs or small groups, wandering with just their
knapsacks through the country, seeking any kind of work
that would give them their daily bread. I often stopped and
talked to them; all felt hopeless about their future. I knew
little about the Nazi movement in the mid-1920s, but by
the end of that decade and the early 1930s it was very much
in evidence. On my brief visits to Germany I saw firsthand
the rise to power of the German Nazis, of Hitler and all the
other Nazi leaders. Munich, a city I had come to love, suddenly seemed full of brown-shirted men, often of arrogant
bearing. In Berlin I stayed by chance at a hotel which was
one of the Nazi gathering spots, especially frequented by
officers and important officials. I sometimes sat for hours
in the hotel lobby, watching and listening to them with
fascination and dread.

The Austrians whom I knew personally at this time were
not political people, and many did not seem to take Nazism
seriously. Of my American friends, some were aware of its
significance, but most were so concerned about the troubles
in the United States after November 1929 that little Austria
and defeated Germany could hardly engage their attention.

This did not surprise me, but I was surprised when, in
August 1932 while spending a few weeks in Russia, I became familiar with the views of a large number of foreign
students in Moscow. My Wellesley friend, whom I have called
Andrea, was living there in a sort of international hostel for
young people, and she introduced me to the others, who
came from all over Europe. They were of course sympathetic
to communism, although rather fearful of the Russian authorities. At the time I did not understand why. Being among
this group was my first experience of having to be careful
and secretive. However, the students—I believe they were
mostly students—accepted me as a friend of Andrea, whom
they trusted.

I spent several evenings with them, some filled with serious talk, some with dancing and singing and feasting on whatever food we were able to get, which was not very much except bread and tea. I brought a few cans of crabmeat and some wine. Whether there were already shops where special things could be bought only with foreign currency or whether the students simply could not afford these delicacies I cannot remember; in any case the crabmeat and wine were a huge success.

I could converse with most of the students in some western European language, and fortunately I knew a little Russian, though not enough for lively talks. But if a Finn or Bulgarian or Hungarian could speak only his own language and Russian, someone could always translate the Russian for me. The thing that absolutely astonished me was that not one of them believed in any Nazi danger! They were convinced that Hitler was an insignificant upstart, that the Nazis were not really Nazis at heart, that Germany was ripe for communism and in six months would have a communist government. (Actually, within seven months Hitler had become chancellor by legal means, and a short time afterwards, chiefly by illegal means, the Nazis were in complete control of Germany.) What I did not realize in Moscow in 1932 was that these students—Europeans, mostly, with a few Americans and perhaps some Asians—had been thoroughly indoctrinated by Communist teaching and had had no opportunity to read or learn anything about the rest of the world. Andrea was certainly a very intelligent young woman, and I believed most of the others to be intelligent also. I could not understand it. The American and British journalists I had met in Moscow were well informed and realistic. In my naïveté, I simply did not know that everything appearing in Russian papers was censored.

I saw and felt in Moscow a wave of hope and optimism that was certainly absent in Germany and many other countries suffering from the Depression. The Russians had work, and most of them seemed to feel that they were working toward a better future. It was not until the beginning of

Stalin's Great Purge following the assassination of Kirov in 1934 that I myself gave up the vacillating feeling of hope which I too had nourished.

The first period of my psychoanalysis was undoubtedly of help to me in spite of the fact that I was always looking forward eagerly to its end. After I had completed three years of analysis—two of them without the customary summer vacation—Dr. Brunswick evidently felt that I had gained all I could and brought my analysis to an end in a most unusual way. I had decided to take a vacation in summer 1929 and was at my last session in late June. After the session was over we shook hands, as was usual in Vienna at the end of every psychoanalytic hour. Dr. Brunswick smilingly wished me a happy summer, and I wished her the same. Then she said good-bye in such a tone of finality that I asked, "Do you mean it's the end? My analysis is over?" Still smiling, she answered "Yes." I was overjoyed. "Oh, how wonderful! I'm so happy!" I exclaimed. Then I remembered to thank her.

During the last year or so I had made new friends in Vienna, mostly students of music or art. Through my piano teacher I met Julian Gardiner, a gifted young Englishman, and we became good friends. Some months after the end of my analysis, Julian and I married. We remained in Vienna so that Julian could continue his studies. Our daughter, Connie, was born there. A few years after our marriage, Julian and I were divorced, and though it caused us both considerable emotional turmoil, it was done amicably, and Julian and I have remained friends. After separating from Julian, I resumed analysis with Dr. Brunswick and immediately became much more wholeheartedly involved than I had been during the first period. Being now deeply interested and convinced that analysis would help me, not only therapeutically but also in doing the educational work to which I still felt committed, I wanted more theoretical training. I began, under Dr. Robert Waelder's superb tutelage, an intensive study of the basic writings of Freud and other analysts. Waelder, a young lay analyst who had been trained originally as a physicist, was one of the best teachers I have ever had as well as a splendid lecturer and public speaker. I read practically all the psychoanalytic writings Freud had produced up to this time, much of Abraham and Ferenczi, and a few other analytic books or papers and talked them over with Waelder for an hour or more twice a week. (In the late 1940s, after Waelder had settled in Philadelphia, I had the pleasure of having professional contact with him there.)

After a year of this work in Vienna, I knew I wanted to train as an analyst, and Dr. Brunswick agreed. I was by no means certain that I wanted to make psychoanalysis my career—I was still set on teaching—but I wanted the training as a psychological foundation for educational work. To complete the training I would need at least some years of practice. Realizing that to practice psychoanalysis in the United States, where I intended to make my home, I would need a medical degree, I reluctantly enrolled in the University of Vienna Medical School in the fall of 1932. I had never been drawn to medicine, and for almost two years I was not sure I would complete the medical course. During this time I did not inform my family that I was studying medicine. When I finally told my mother, she had a hard time believing it. My sister had studied medicine immediately after college, and although my mother did not oppose it she did not encourage it either. But Mother had completely identified my interests with literature and the arts and had hoped and believed I would become a writer.

I continued my work with Waelder on a one-to-one basis, then had the same sort of private hours with Siegfried Bernfeld and August Aichhorn, with whom I concentrated chiefly on the psychology of adolescents. Later I became one of a group of four American women meeting about once a week with each of these two excellent teachers. In this small group we spoke English; probably the Americans were not all sufficiently familiar with German. It helped me to gain a psychoanalytic vocabulary in both languages. I did not go to any larger psychoanalytic classes—did not even know whether any existed—except for one taught by Aichhorn at the university. (It was at one of these lectures that I first saw, though I did not meet, young Kurt Eissler, who later became one of my most helpful and most cherished friends. I admired him at that moment because he boldly went up to the platform in front of the class to demonstrate some point and make diagrams on the blackboard.)

I was never really part of the psychoanalytic community until my last few years in Vienna, when I was invited to attend the famous Wednesday evening meetings. Although Freud could no longer be present, the meetings were nevertheless rightly judged famous, attended by analysts whose names are now among the best known and most highly appreciated in the world—among them Anna Freud, Dorothy Burlingham, Paul Federn, the Krises, the Bibrings, the Waelders, Helene Deutsch, Jeanne Lampl-de Groot, Ruth Mack Brunswick, Sigfried Bernfeld, Berta Bornstein, and the Sterbas. The papers presented and the discussions following them were so stimulating that often I could not sleep for hours later.

About the time I began medical school I became more concerned with Austrian politics. With the rapid growth and spread of Nazism in Germany, the Nazis became more evident not only in the Austrian provinces but also in Vienna. Anti-Semitism was far from new in Vienna, and before I entered medical school, perhaps long before, it was well known that, of the two anatomy divisions in two different wings of the anatomy building, one section was attended by Jews and Socialists, the other by Christian Socialists and anti-Semites. Now it became clear that many in the latter section were Nazis. They frequently attempted to raid the Socialist section and were sometimes violent. I remember my first such experience: I was sitting at a long dissection table with several other American students, all Jewish, when one of them shouted in English, "They're coming, the Nazis

are coming! Get your knives ready!" Somehow this did not
result in a bloody battle, but there were other times (when
I did not happen to be present) when Jewish students were
injured and even thrown out of windows.

The great world economic crisis did not spare Austria. In
the spring of 1931 Austria's greatest banking house, the Cre-
ditanstalt, went bankrupt, bringing Austria close to financial and economic disaster. The result was even more support
for the Nazis. Provincial elections showed that the Nazis
were gaining votes from the conservative parties. The Heimwehr, formerly the "army" of the Christian Socialists, now
considered itself a party modeled on the Italian Fascists and
was pressing the Christian Socialists to take the offensive
against the Social Democrats. A series of constitutional
amendments had given the president increased powers, no-
tably to appoint ministers and to issue emergency decrees.
Vienna, however, preserved its autonomy against the au-
thoritarian demands of the Heimwehr. After the Austrian
elections in May 1932, Engelbert Dollfuss as chancellor
formed a Christian Socialist government in which he could
count on a majority in parliament of only one vote. Feeling
threatened by both the Nazis and the Social Democrats,
Dollfuss determined to replace the parliament by an au-
thoritarian system and seized the opportunity to do so when
the president and two vice-presidents of the lower house of
parliament resigned. Dollfuss, declaring that parliamentary
government had proved unworkable, thenceforth governed
by emergency decree. This happened in March 1933, when,
with Hitler in power in Germany, Nazi propaganda to in-
corporate Austria was increasing. Dollfuss, relying on the
Heimwehr and its Italian Fascist contacts, turned to Italy
for help. (He knew he could not count on France and England.) In the summer of 1933 he visited Mussolini, hoping
to get his promise to protect Austria. Mussolini agreed on
the condition that Dollfuss would give the Heimwehr a free
hand in the destruction of the Austrian Social Democratic
Party. The deal was made. That same year Dollfuss founded

the Vaterländische Front ("Fatherland Front"), which united all conservative groups and eventually became Austria's only legal party.

I began at about this time to consider leaving Austria in the summer of 1934, when I would have completed the two preclinical years at the Vienna Medical School. It would be a logical time to transfer to an American medical school, which I thought would probably accept me as a second-year student. Even so, the entire course would not take longer since American training lasted four years instead of the Austrian five-and-a-half to six. I believed I would get better training in the United States, or at least that I would work better under the American system. If I wanted to continue my analysis and Dr. Brunswick remained in Vienna, I would have to transfer to someone in the United States.

Perhaps behind this whole train of logical thinking lurked the feeling that I did not really want to live in a Fascist country, especially with the Nazis just around the corner.

Two

From Muriel to "Mary": Vienna, from Spring 1934 until the Anschluss

The Fascist assault on the Social Democrats changed all my plans. I knew without a shadow of doubt that I wanted to remain in Vienna doing all I could to keep the spark of democracy alive despite Austria's Fascist dictatorship.

During the spring of 1934, underground work occupied only a small portion of my time. My daily life continued much as before: medical school, psychoanalysis, frequent weekends with my three-year-old daughter, Connie, at our little cottage at Sulz in the Vienna Woods, occasional concerts, visits with a few friends. In late April, during the spring vacation, I decided I wanted to get away for two weeks. Connie, Gerda—her governess, who had had training as a kindergarten teacher in one of the schools influenced by Anna Freud—and I took a boat down the Dalmatian coast to Mlini, a small village not far from Dubrovnik. After a few days there I was to continue down the coast to Greece while Connie and Gerda remained at a little inn I had chosen outside the village. I had selected this spot from various circulars because it was the only one that advertized a sand beach. The proprietor, replying to my various inquiries, told me that two distinguished English journalists who had been staying at the inn for several weeks were enchanted with it. I pictured two elderly gentlemen in tweed jackets, each with a pipe, sitting quietly with their newspapers or walking briskly through the olive groves.

This simple and attractive inn, situated on a small, curved beach, was just what we wanted. On our way in to dinner the first night, the proprietor introduced us to his two English guests, who in no way resembled the elderly journalists I had pictured. They seemed about twenty-five years of age, very friendly and informal, and attractive in both appearance and manner. One, whose name I had understood to be Spender or Spencer, was indeed strikingly handsome, very tall and well built with a slight tendency to stoop, probably because of his height. He had curly fair hair and round, intensely blue eyes. His expression was youthfully idealistic but at the same time a little sad. His companion, less striking but very personable, charmed me at once with his open, friendly face and ready smile. His neat, well-proportioned body with its natural ease of movement suggested a graceful animal. After dinner, when we talked together, I asked their names, which the proprietor had slurred over. "Are you Mr. Spender?" I inquired of the taller one. "He's *Stephen* Spender, the poet," his companion said proudly. "I'm Tony Hyndman, his secretary." I did not admit that I had never heard of Stephen Spender, who in fact had published mostly in magazines I was not familiar with.

Stephen and I liked each other immediately and found we had many interests in common. We had both been at Oxford, although not at the same time, and we shared similar reservations about it. We knew and loved many of the same places in Europe. Our tastes in art, music, and literature were congenial. Most important, Stephen was passionately concerned with the political situation in Germany and Austria and eager to learn all he could about the events of February and the underground movement. The two men were thinking of coming to Vienna in early summer.

Connie was, as always, enchanted with the sea and the

sand, and I felt comfortable leaving her and Gerda in this delightful spot while I continued my journey down the coast as far as Piraeus on a small, leisurely cargo ship. It was late April, the air was warm, and I slept on deck. At each port of call I explored the little town, sat at an outdoor café watching the people, and usually had a swim. After spending a few days in Athens, I returned by a larger ship which stopped only at Dubrovnik, where Connie and Gerda joined me. We were back in Vienna in early May.

I had decided, the previous autumn, to return to America in the summer of 1934, when I would have completed two years of medicine at the University of Vienna, and transfer to an American medical school. Now, however, becoming ever more involved in the underground movement and certain that I could be useful, I reconsidered. I felt I simply could not leave. This work meant more to me at the time than medicine or psychoanalysis or living in America.

I had unfortunately given notice, before February, that I would vacate my apartment in the Frankgasse by August. Immediately I set to work trying to get it back. This proved to be impossible; the apartment had been "sold" to another client. Perhaps if I had been more experienced in bribery I could have done something about it. But, difficult as finding another apartment and inconvenient as moving would be, the change offered one possible advantage. The concierge and his wife at Frankgasse 1 were untrustworthy and even violent people. I had often heard them drunkenly shouting and quarreling in their loge at the entrance to the building; once I had seen the woman chasing her husband with a kitchen knife. I knew they spied on the apartment owners and on everyone who came into the building, and I had good reason to believe they had poisoned my dog. I had no doubt that, if they became suspicious of the Kulczars and others who came to my apartment, they would attempt to blackmail me or turn me over to the police.

Apartments were extremely scarce and difficult to obtain, and my search was time-consuming and wearisome. At length

I settled on a flat that seemed suitable in many respects but was definitely too small. It was in a pleasant new building in the Rummelhardtgasse, opposite the General Hospital and close to the clinics and lecture halls, so the location could not have been better. But, as it had only three rooms, I would have to sleep in the living-dining room and would have little privacy. I could not study there without forbidding Connie to enter my room, which I was unwilling to do. As I had always done some of my studying in a coffee-house, I supposed I could manage. But I wished I could rent an additional separate room where I could work in solitude, near enough for me to return home quickly if needed.

And then I had the greatest stroke of luck. My friend Felix Augenfeld, whom we called "Auge," an architect who had helped to improve my first apartment and who had built our little cottage in Sulz, wanted to move to a Vienna suburb and was looking for someone to sublet his apartment in the Lammgasse, about five minutes' walk from the place I had just rented in the Rummelhardtgasse. I was acquainted with the apartment, which consisted of a large studio and a small bedroom, bath, and kitchenette. It was on the top floor overlooking a courtyard surrounded by lower buildings, so no one could see into the windows. An additional advantage, for conspiratorial purposes, was that the concierge's loge—unlike almost every other—was not at the entrance to the building but at the rear, out of sight of even the stairs and elevator. It seemed a gift from heaven. The apartment would remain in Auge's name; he would continue to have all dealings with the landlord and take care of any other matters that might arise. It had a telephone and a convenient heating and hot-water system. I could not have asked for anything better, or nearly so good. Auge also was delighted, and we promptly completed the arrangements. By June everything was set for the coming September, when the actual moving would take place.

Now that the immediate emergency following the February struggle was over, I tried to prevent my underground comrades from coming to my apartment, but I still saw the Kulczars there and at their apartment. We had of course arranged some plausible story as to how we knew each other in case we should be questioned, and we took precautions not to be followed when going to one another's home or any other meeting place. The conspiratorial rules they taught me were excellent; only months later, however, I realized that they themselves were not following the rules.

I did have one more secret visitor during the spring of 1934 at the Frankgasse, referred to me by someone I trusted. I had by telephone given this visitor an appointment for a Sunday morning when I expected to be alone in the apartment while Connie and Gerda were on an all-day excursion in the Wiener Wald. It was a beautiful day, with the sun pouring in through the open windows of my living room. My visitor arrived punctually, an extremely handsome, dark-haired man, probably younger than I, dressed in hiking clothes and boots and carrying a rucksack. He spoke impeccable English, and I felt he must have been educated at an English school. But I was not certain of his national origin, for his occasional German phrases also had an authentic ring. We talked cautiously at first as we drank our coffee and as he smoked or played with his pipe. We got into a rather theoretical discussion of politics, which gradually led into broader areas of history, sociology, philosophy. I was fascinated by my guest's intelligence and charm. After about two hours' talk neither of us showed an inclination to stop, so I made some sandwiches and more coffee and we continued our discussion well into the afternoon. I remained mystified as to who this man was, his nationality and party, whether he was living in Vienna or simply passing through, and whether he would want some service from me after he had explored my attitude sufficiently. I was of course reticent about my underground work and connections but frank in stating my socialist affiliations. At that time I was open-minded to communism, sharing many of its stated goals but critical of its methods, and I let him know this also. He did not commit himself. I had not met with such complete secrecy before, and it made me somewhat uneasy. In all other respects my hours with this curious visitor were very enjoyable and I hoped to get to know him better.

As he stood up to leave, my guest, evidently satisfied with my credentials, asked me if I would be willing to deliver an envelope of money to a "comrade." (*Genosse*, the German word for comrade, was used equally by Socialists and Communists.) I said I would. I was to go to a certain tram stop on a busy street at two o'clock the following afternoon, carrying the envelope of money inside the daily newspaper. A man, who was described to me in minute detail as to appearance, clothing, and a special sign of identification, would come up to me and ask a particular question, such as which tram to take to a certain railway station. I was to answer in specific, prearranged words and then give him the newspaper containing the envelope. My guest asked me what I would be wearing; then he opened his rucksack and took out a large, sealed manila envelope. I was surprised at the size of it, expecting a normal-sized envelope containing, probably, a few hundred-schilling notes, but I had neither the experience nor the presence of mind to ask to see the contents. We shook hands and said a friendly Auf Wiedersehen.

As the day wore on I became more and more uneasy about the big envelope. It must contain a great deal of money, I thought. I debated long with myself about whether I had the right to open it, and at last I decided I would do so. This was not altogether logical, since I supposed I would deliver the money no matter what the sum. I opened the envelope. In it there were indeed several thousand schillings, but the bulk of the contents was clandestine Communist literature. I felt betrayed and was all the more angry for having so readily succumbed to the charms of a man I knew nothing about.

At exactly two o'clock on Monday I was at the designated

street corner, but my contact did not appear. I waited uneasily, having learned that punctuality is the first rule of conspiracy. I began to reproach myself for not having burned the literature and brought only the money to deliver. Twenty-five minutes passed. I decided I would wait just five minutes more, then return home, destroy the literature, and keep the money until someone contacted me. At that moment a young man of the given description politely asked me which tram to take to the Franz Josef Station. I answered as arranged, handed him the newspaper containing the envelope, and stepped into a tram that was loading at that moment. Fortunately it took me away from home; I wanted to make several changes in order to check whether I was being followed. At length I arrived home, bitterly angry at these two men who had deceived and endangered me, and determined never to see the unidentified caller again. He had probably had this same idea all the time, in spite of the cordial Auf Wiedersehen, for I never heard from him again.

More than thirty years later, while visiting friends in Connecticut, I happened to pick up a book by E. H. Cookridge: *The Third Man*, a biography of Kim Philby. The author, who had spent his childhood and youth in Vienna, where his father represented a Manchester textile firm, had been a member of the Social Democratic Club at the University of Vienna and later became a newspaper reporter. After February 1934, Cookridge became engaged in Socialist underground work and met Kim Philby, who was in Vienna from summer 1933 to summer 1934.

One day, Cookridge writes,* Philby came to him offering to provide "a safe house" for meetings of the Socialist Central Committee. The house was owned by an Englishwoman "known as 'Mary' (her real name was Muriel Gardiner). . . . She made her flats available for illegal meetings; the garden sheds at her villa were soon filled with stacks of clandestine

*E. H. Cookridge, *The Third Man* (New York: G. P. Putnam's, Berkley Medallion, 1968), p. 32.

news-sheets and pamphlets. . . ." According to Cookridge, Philby had "pretended" that he had enlisted Mary to work for the Socialists, but it was soon found out that in fact Mary had been "discovered" by Ilse Kulczar. "I assume," writes Cookridge, "that Kim Philby had good reasons of his own to pose as go-between. Also, as I had already then discovered, while helping the Socialist groups he was at the same time involved with our opponents, the Communist organizations."

In spite of gross inaccuracies (there were a number of others besides the "stacks of clandestine news-sheets" and the equally nonexistent "garden sheds") I had no doubt that I was the "Mary" Philby talked about, and I tried to figure out when and in what circumstances Philby could have known me. And then I recalled my unknown visitor as the only likely possibility. Yet I could not be certain; my recollection of him did not at all tally with the picture I formed in my mind while reading about Philby, the notorious double agent. I could not wait to check and as soon as possible went into a bookshop to look for other biographies of Philby. In the first one I picked up I found a photograph of Philby as a young man—he was indeed my handsome, charming, trust-inspiring guest of spring 1934.

Toward the end of May I received a letter from Stephen Spender saying that he and Tony would be arriving in Vienna that week. I was surprised at how pleased, even excited, I was; I already liked Stephen very much. However, the reason for their coming earlier than planned was not a happy one: Tony had not been well and wanted better medical attention than he could get in a Yugoslavian village. Could I recommend a doctor?

By the time they had arrived two days later I had already made a doctor's appointment for Tony, and he entered the hospital within a few days. I invited Stephen to stay in our apartment during Tony's hospitalization and asked Tony to join us there for his convalescence. The operation was without complications but, as was the practice then, Tony had to stay a rather long time in the hospital. Stephen and I visited him every day but had time to do many things together and had long talks almost every evening. We quickly grew to know each other well and were soon in love. Stephen was perfectly open about the fact that his previous relationships had been only with men. I remember his saying, before making love to me the first time, "I'm a little embarrassed. You see, I've never been in love with a woman before, never even been attracted to a woman." We were both concerned about hurting Tony. The fact that we could all speak openly and sincerely about this and that we all felt true friendship for one another made the situation less difficult than one might expect.

The following two months, until I left for a vacation in France, were packed indeed, with both an intense personal life and dramatic political events. Stephen and Tony spent much of this time in my cottage in Sulz, and although I usually had to be in Vienna on weekdays I sometimes went out for an evening, and Connie and I spent most weekends there. I remember going to Sulz after Hitler's June 30 purge of Roehm and other S.A. leaders in Germany to bring Stephen the newspapers and the latest radio reports. On July 26, the day after the Nazis' assassination of Austrian Chancellor Engelbert Dollfuss, I again brought the news to Sulz, this time with Connie. As we drove the length of the Mariahilferstrasse, with its buildings majestically draped in black, I told Connie that this was an important day to remember and explained to her as well as I could what had happened and the political background of the assassination.

I think neither Stephen nor I was ever able really to escape from these fateful events and our fears of a doomed future. We did not try to escape. But, even though we could not be carefree, we were happy in our love and understanding of each other and in our mutual dedication to the cause of freedom. We were happy also in the beauty of the woods and the mountains, in our love of poetry, and—although we did not recognize it in those words—in enjoying youth and health and energy.

In early August we all left Vienna, I to go with Connie and Gerda to Juan-les-Pins, on the French Riviera, to spend a month with Helen and Joe Furnas. I had known Helen slightly when we were children in Chicago, at the same school but in different grades. When years later we met by chance in Oxford, we became firm friends. I had a part in introducing her to Joe Furnas when he had just had his first article accepted by a newspaper.*

It gave me great satisfaction when, before I left Vienna, the Kulczars indicated that they wanted me to become a member of the small Central Committee that would form the policy and organize the activities of the Funke group. I suppose in some way I felt I had earned my vacation.

It was good to be away from my immediate problems. Juan-les-Pins was not yet the overcrowded tourist spot it has since become. We stayed in a small, pleasant pension, close to the beach, where Connie could spend the entire day. Helen, Joe, and I would work in the mornings. I slaved over my big anatomy books; Joe and Helen were busy writing. We would all spend the afternoon on the beach or occasionally make some excursion. In the evenings Helen, Joe, and I would sit in a café or pavilion at the water's edge, talking, laughing, and solving complicated literary crossword puzzles. To be with such relaxing yet stimulating friends, concerned about the tragedies of the world but not quite in the midst of them, was just what I most needed. And Connie and I were always happiest and closest on vacations, when I was not distracted by responsibilities and worries, and especially happy at the sea, which we both loved.

By the end of August I was physically and mentally rested and ready to return to Vienna. On the way, however, Connie, Gerda, and I were to stop for a few days at Lucerne,

*This had been the beginning of a successful. career; as J. C. Furnas he has written histories, biographies, and essays.

where the International Psychoanalytic Congress was being held. Gladys Lack was to meet us there and return with us to Vienna.

This was the first Psychoanalytic Congress I had ever attended, and I felt completely lost and out of place. A few of the analysts there had been my teachers, but I revered them from a distance and hardly dared talk with them. I was not a member of any students' group since most of my study with experienced analysts had been on an individual basis. I knew distantly a number of analysts who were parents of children Connie played with—the Krises, the Waelders, the Kubies, the Bibrings, and others—but I was much too shy to approach them. It was Grete Bibring who, probably recognizing my shyness, took me under her wing and made the conference tolerable for me.

I was glad when it was over and we were on the night train to Vienna. We spent our first days in Vienna getting settled in the new apartment in the Rummelhardtgasse. (The apartment in the Lammgasse, my workroom, would not be available for a little while yet.) The furniture was hardly set up, much less arranged satisfactorily, when Stephen and Tony arrived. We put mattresses on the floor and somehow or other all squeezed in.

I had of course told Gladys about Stephen and Tony, but she was not prepared for their friendliness, informality, and charm. Most of the Englishmen Gladys and I had known at Oxford had been aloof and either arrogant or overly shy. "Stephen's rather breathtakingly beautiful," Gladys said to me when we had a moment alone. Together we spent some lovely September days in Sulz, taking long walks through the woods, picking the fragrant little wild cyclamen that enchanted us all. Cooking our meals in Sulz was always hilarious, as none of us knew much about cooking and the facilities were very limited. I usually made the main dish— some extraordinary combination of meat or eggs or cheese together with fruit or some interesting condiment—on the little kerosene stove in the kitchen, when I could make it work. The others would concoct some surprise side dish, such as chestnuts or roasted apples, in the fireplace. The one standard dish, which we always had when Connie was with us, was cream of wheat with grated chocolate; it was her favorite, and it rapidly became a favorite of ours, too. When Gerda was with us, she would make an excellent Wiener schnitzel and sometimes Knödel, a sort of fluffy dumpling.

In Vienna I was busy getting settled, seeing friends, and studying several hours a day in a coffeehouse. The university term had not yet begun and my analyst had not yet returned from her vacation, so my day was fairly flexible. Evenings we might go to the opera or a concert or just walk around the Vienna streets, perhaps drop into a café or a wine cellar, and talk and talk. Gladys left after a week or two; Stephen and Tony stayed somewhat longer.

Of course I saw the Kulczars frequently, and then the day arrived for my first meeting with the Funke Central Committee. (Earlier, before I joined the Central Committee of the splinter group Funke, I had allowed the Central Committee of the entire Socialist party to meet at Sulz, so I had met its leaders—Leichter, Pollak, Sailer, Holoubek, Ackermann, and others whom I later knew well—but as I was not a member I had kept out of their way during the meeting.) At the Funke meeting, besides the Kulczars and myself there were five other members, two of whom I had already met through Poldi. One of these was Karl Hartl, the "Hermann" of the cell I had visited the previous spring, an outgoing young man who spoke so fast and with such a strong Viennese accent that I had difficulty following him. The other was an inconspicuous young woman named Elly Herzfeld, whose cover-name was "Hertha." She was getting her doctorate in psychology at the university and I soon learned that she was an extremely intelligent, serious person. Since we were both at the university and obviously had interests in common, it was agreed that our acquaintance should be "legal"—in other words, we were to acknowledge being friends and meet openly.

Of the three I was meeting for the first time, Karl Czernitz, whom we called "Thomas," made little impression on me, and I never got to know him well. Peter Kalischer, "Cornelius," was the oldest of the group, in his late forties or early fifties. He had a dark, unsmiling, intelligent face, a concise and brilliant way of speaking, and altogether a magnetic personality. I was immediately drawn to him and wanted to know more about him.

Very different in appearance and manner was Joseph Buttinger, "Wieser," as we called him. (He had a series of covernames and wrote illegal articles under the name of Gustav Richter.) He was very quiet at this meeting, being new to the group except for his brief acquaintance with the Kulczars. I tried to judge him by his face: open, energetic, receptive, uncomplicated, and above all honest. After studying Wieser's, I looked again at the others' faces and realized that not one of them struck me as appearing equally honest. Even at this first meeting it occurred to me to wonder whether it was rare for honest people to go into illegal work. Or did illegal work itself reduce one's appearance of honesty? Then I wondered how my face looked to the others. Would they describe it as honest? I suspected no one would even think of the question, except possibly Hertha.

The meeting, held in the Kulczars' living room on a Sunday morning, lasted several hours. General policy of the group was mapped out, and conspiracy rules were stressed. I left the meeting feeling stimulated and encouraged; at last, after seven months, I had found where I belonged in the underground.

During the next two months, we held an occasional full committee meeting at the Sulz cottage. This was a treat for everyone; it was such a joy to get into the glorious autumn sunlight in this enchanting spot; furthermore, we felt safe there. The cottage—in a meadow sloping down to the road and surrounded on the other three sides by woods—was a full mile from the village or from any other house. The few people I knew in the village were familiar with the fact that I had many guests, especially on weekends. Nothing about these get-togethers would arouse suspicion. We could relax and laugh together and still get on with our deadly serious business.

The Funke group sometimes met in my new apartment in the Lammgasse. I was often there alone to study, especially in the evening, but I invited no guests except, occasionally, Augenfeld. Connie and Gerda knew the telephone number but not the address. Most of my friends knew I had a place where I could study absolutely undisturbed but knew neither the address nor the telephone number. It was an ideal place for me to meet one or more or all of the committee members.

Hertha and I grew to know each other fairly well. I liked and trusted her. She had had a sad life and was often depressed, but this never interfered with her efficiency. She told me about her friends, a group of five or six girls who had attended the same private high school and had gone on together to the university. Every one of them, including herself, was, according to Hertha, neurotic and unhappy. One of them, Kaethe Wolf, who became a psychologist, I later knew in America.

The member of the group whom I was most interested in knowing better was Cornelius. He seemed the most brilliant and was always listened to when he spoke. And yet, after the third or fourth meeting, I became suspicious that something was wrong about him. He was frequently late to meetings or did not come at all, and he would offer elaborate—too elaborate—excuses, always with a touch of the dramatic. At one meeting he was supposed to report on a trip to Czechoslovakia, where he was to have contacted some of the old party members. He had been given money from the Funke treasury to pay for this trip. But at the meeting he told us in his quiet but dramatic voice that on the way

to the station he had been robbed of this money and of all
his own money as well. Without even carfare in his pocket,
he had had to walk two hours back to his home. He had had
to borrow a few schillings to be able to come to this meeting. Now he asked for and was given a small loan to tide
him over the next week or so. I don't know what the others
thought, but I simply did not believe him.

Shortly afterward, Cornelius asked to borrow my typewriter while his was being repaired. I told him I needed it
and could not spare it for long. He assured me he would
return it within a week and pleaded with me to let him have
it for some very urgent typing he had to do. I gave in. Of
course it was not returned within a week or within several
weeks. During this period Hertha spoke to me of Cornelius.
He had a very sick wife, who not only could not work but
needed a good deal of money for medication and other medical expenses. The Krankenkasse, or Austrian insurance system, took care of no more than the barest essentials. Cornelius
worked only sporadically—doing what I can't remember—
but he and his wife were really close to starving. Hertha
knew these details not directly but from a friend, Isa Strasser. Isa, with her husband, Josef Strasser, a well-known political worker and writer, had lived for some years in Russia,
after which, disillusioned with Communism, they had returned to Vienna and become ardent Socialists.

Hertha told me that Isa wanted to talk to me about Cornelius and that, in any case, she thought Isa and I would
like to know each other. I met Isa soon after and we got on
well together from the first. She told me more about Cornelius, much of which I have now forgotten. He was a courageous, gifted, altogether valuable person who had done
much for his political cause. But he was now in debt to
everyone who could lend him money. Isa herself, who had
two children and a dying husband, had already lent him
more than she could afford. I mentioned my typewriter. "I'm
sure he's pawned it," said Isa. "He's already pawned his own
and mine and everything else he could spare. Now he has

to pawn something else, to pay the monthly interest on all those pawn tickets. You'll never get your typewriter back." She wanted to know whether I could give Cornelius any work or help him find any; she assured me that he was a hard worker and reliable in that respect. It occurred to me that Cornelius might give me some lessons in economics and political science, particularly Marxism. I was painfully ignorant of the basic tenets of Marxism, since I had never studied it, and had never progressed very far in my occasional attempts to instruct myself.

It was arranged that Cornelius should come to me at the Rummelhardtgasse two evenings a week. I found him a brilliant teacher, as I had expected, and thoroughly enjoyed the lessons. After a time, though, they became complicated by his personal problems, some of which were based on reality and some inherent in his character. He talked frequently of suicide. I felt that although he was serious about it, at the same time he wanted me to persuade him to give up the idea. However, I kept my role to that of listener, feeling that to give any advice might be dangerous. He told me one evening that he had thought of joining Mussolini's army in the hope that he would get killed. This fantastic, contradictory idea—that a devoted Socialist should by choice join and fight for the Fascists—was characteristic of Cornelius, dramatic and desperate as he was. I did not argue with him; I just told him, rather brutally, "You'll have to decide."

Cornelius stayed longer than usual the evening of this exchange. Half an hour after he left, he called me from a pay station. "I'm going to kill myself," he said. "I can't go on. I shall do it now. I have a gun." My questions to him met with silence. I was convinced I would hear the report of a gun in a moment. I began to argue. "You can't do that," I said. "Certainly not without careful preparation. You would get us all into trouble. The police would investigate and they'd find out you had just left my apartment. I'm sure I'd be arrested. And they would link you to our other friends also. You can't do this to us."

At length he spoke. "I'll wait," he said.

Cornelius did not commit suicide. Nor did he go to Ethiopia to be killed. Instead, he lived in Vienna until 1938, when the Nazis interned him at Dachau, where he perished. Comrades who survived him tell of his noble demeanor there; he worked hard, generously helped the other victims, taught them, encouraged them, never lamented. He was loved and admired by all. Poor brilliant, sometimes untrustworthy, suffering, noble Cornelius.

Naturally I was getting to know the Kulczars better as I became more active in underground work. One conversation with Poldi disturbed me greatly. He told me of a comrade whom he suspected of being disloyal, though I do not remember what had aroused his suspicions. "If it is true," he concluded, "we shall have to put him out of the way." My blood ran cold, partly because of the words Poldi used, partly because of the expression on his face and in his voice as he spoke them—a mixture of cruelty and pleasure. I was too much taken aback to question him further; I think I had not the courage to do so. I wanted to give the matter more thought. Was my instant revulsion justified? Was Poldi's conclusion a logical necessity in a violent, dictatorial world? I thought a great deal about this, and I still do. My feeling of revulsion remains. But does this feeling get in the way of clear thinking? Can we rely on universal moral laws, or must each case be judged individually?

In late November I learned that the Kulczars were in trouble. Unknown to me and to most of our comrades, they had flagrantly broken a conspiratorial rule: they had assigned the job of courier between Vienna and Brno to a young man who was the fiancé of their maid. The Austrian police caught the fellow carrying money, messages, and illegal literature, and his connection with the Kulczars led the authorities directly to them. Poldi and Ilse fled at once to St. Pölten, where an uninvolved friend of Hermann's would shelter them for a few days. They would escape to Czechoslovakia as soon as they could obtain false passports, which they would wait for in an obscure little inn in the mountains, about two hours from Vienna.

It was Hermann who brought me the devastating news. He was already at work trying to find passports of nonpolitical friends whose descriptions would match Poldi's and Ilse's; then it would be necessary to exchange photographs and get the passports restamped to complete the transformation. All this would take several days. Hermann asked me to deliver the passports as soon as they were completed to the Kulczars at the inn. I said I would.

Hermann brought me the passports on a Thursday morning. (I believe it was our American Thanksgiving holiday.) I had to attend a required laboratory period that afternoon, but we agreed that no time was to be lost. I would leave directly after lab and, if necessary, stay the night at the mountain inn. Hermann told me to take a train to Gloggnitz, about an hour south of Vienna. At the station there I would find a bus that would take me to the inn.

I packed a rucksack with a few necessities, putting the passports at the bottom of my toilet-article bag. It was a cold, dark November afternoon, so I dressed in warm clothes and a poncho. I arrived in Gloggnitz at about six o'clock. The rain was coming down hard. No bus would be going to the inn or anywhere near it until noon the next day, but there was one, scheduled to leave shortly, that would take me to its end-station, three or four miles along the road. I thought of taking a taxi up the mountain but knew that would be too conspicuous. I also thought of staying overnight in Gloggnitz but feared the risk of a wasted day to the Kulczars. I decided I would have to walk from the end-station to the inn.

The bus took me a short distance up the mountain and dropped me off at a pleasant-looking restaurant in the woods. I went in and ordered dinner and a glass of wine, then inquired of the waiter the distance to the inn. "Drei Gehstunden"—a three-hour walk—he replied. "You won't want to try it tonight, Miss, in this downpour. And it's probably

snowing higher up." I did not comment on this but ascer-
tained that the road was the same one I had just traveled on
the bus and that there were no forks or side roads to worry
about. One had simply to continue up and up.

Warmed and somewhat comforted by the heated room
and good food, I started out. The night was pitch black. Rain
poured steadily down; fortunately there was no wind. I was
frightened—without good reason, since it was unlikely that
anything untoward would befall me. Perhaps I was just afraid
of being alone in the dark in an unknown terrain, though I
had never before been afraid of the dark. It was not hard to
keep to the road since it was flanked by woods on both sides.
I was thankful there were no precipices.

After I had walked for perhaps an hour—I could not see
my watch—I heard heavy footsteps coming down the mountain toward me, and I became even more frightened. Then
the person approaching began to whistle, which reassured
me somewhat. As we passed he greeted me with "Grüss
Gott," and I replied "Grüss Gott." This was my only en-
counter during the wearisome climb.

At last I saw lights shining ahead of me. They came from
the inn, and to my relief the proprietor was still up. I registered in my own name, supposing that some identification
would be required. But I did not know in what name the
Kulczars were registered and in any case thought it best not
to ask for them. I would have to wait until morning, when
we could meet by chance. But knowing that the bus I hoped
we would take down to Gloggnitz would be calling at the
inn about ten, and knowing the Kulczars' tendency to sleep
late, I was a little worried. I decided to try to make my
presence known, at the risk of disturbing whatever other
guests might be lodging at the inn.

"Could I have some bread and cheese and something hot
to drink?" I asked in German in an abnormally loud voice,
exaggerating my American accent. "I'll just take off my wet
coat and boots and sit a while in your warm dining room,"
I added. I had seen that the inn—it was more like a ski hut—

was very small and that the partitions between the rooms were flimsy. There was a good chance the Kulczars would hear me and recognize my voice and accent. I went into the dining room, determined to draw my host into further loud conversation when he brought my tea. But before he returned, Poldi and Ilse had joined me, excited, laughing, and friendly. I thought it unwise to show that we were old friends, but again their conspiratorial technique had deserted them. Apparently there were no other guests at the inn, and we talked quietly for a few minutes; then I took Ilse into my room and gave her the passports.

In the morning we checked out and took the bus to Gloggnitz and then a train to Vienna. Poldi and Ilse got out at a local station on the outskirts and from there caught a streetcar to the station in Vienna and boarded the train for Brno. I continued on to the terminal, taking the precaution of traveling by two trams and a taxi to my apartment.

I don't remember much about the following month. New arrangements for making contact with the group had to be worked out. It was usually Hertha or Hermann who contacted me, but Wieser came a few times alone to my workroom to give me messages for others. He was working chiefly in the provinces. Once when he came to tell me he was about to start on a trip, it occurred to me to ask him whether he had enough money. "Oh, yes," he replied cheerfully. "I always keep an extra thirty schillings in my pocket." This astonished me, as the others were always completely broke.

I was at this time working hard at anatomy, histology, and physiology, as I was to take examinations in these subjects during the next semester. In the dissection class it was the custom for a team of six students to work together on three or more cadavers in succession. I was a member of a team of very bright and interesting students, including Gretl Hitschmann, daughter of the psychoanalyst Eduard Hitschmann, who herself later became an analyst, and Harold Harvey, an American. In October I discovered that Harold and I lived in the same building in the Rummelhardtgasse.

Until that time I had known him only through contacts in medical school, and we were rather shy with each other. But we both seemed to be lonely, so I invited him to spend Christmas Eve with us. Harold, Connie, and I had dinner together; after Connie had gone to bed, Harold and I trimmed her Christmas tree. It was the beginning of a life-long friendship. Twenty-one years later Harold and Connie married.

Stephen came to Vienna for the month of January. I was studying and he was writing, but we had time for other things too. We went to Brno for a few days, taking messages to and from the Kulczars. There we met Otto Bauer, the leader of the Austrian Socialists in exile. My code name, Mary, had to be changed, and, making some joking reference to Queen Mary and Queen Elizabeth, Bauer christened me Elizabeth. But Mary I remained for most of my friends in Austria.

The days I remember with the most joy during this month were those Stephen and I spent at the cottage in Sulz, days of intimate conversation in front of the open fire or of skiing the gentle snowy slopes. Although we did not dream of it at the time, this was to be our last month as lovers.

It must have been shortly after Stephen left that Hermann sought me out to tell me that Wieser had had to go underground. He asked whether Wieser, as soon as he returned from a short trip in the provinces, could spend a week or so at Sulz, where he would grow a mustache in an attempt to change his appearance.

This was probably in early February, just when I was most involved in preparing for my examinations. However, I arranged to be at Sulz for the first two days of Wieser's stay. After that he would remain there alone. On the appointed day, I took a late afternoon bus which, as always, let me off at a stop about a hundred yards in front of the cottage, to which I climbed by a wooded path. The first thing to do this snowy winter's day was to light the stove that warmed the whole house, then unpack the food I had brought in my knapsack, pump some water, begin to cook, and finally light the open fire. I had just completed these chores when Wieser knocked at the door, having taken a later bus to the crossroads a half-mile beyond the cottage and walked back.

Of all the Funke group, I knew Wieser least well, except for Thomas. Wanting him to feel very comfortable and at ease, as I shook his ice-cold hand I covered it for an instant with my left hand. I had intended this as a welcoming gesture—but I think I felt the first erotic spark pass between us at that moment.

After supper, sitting on the couch in front of the open fire, we talked and talked. We knew nothing of each other except that we shared the same political views. How much there was to tell of our so different lives! And how easy it was to talk, by the firelight in this cozy room, so safe and far from the Vienna police and that dreaded knock at the door. Wieser told me how at six in the morning some weeks earlier the police came to his room, rented in his own name, after he and many other Socialists had attended a conference in Brno. Most of the members of the outlawed party had been arrested, but Wieser talked the police into thinking he was innocent. He left the apartment immediately after his interrogator did—just half an hour before the police returned.

Then he began to tell me about his childhood.

His father was one of twelve children of a small farmer in Upper Austria, his mother an orphan working on a farm in the village of Reichersbeuern in Bavaria. In the spring of 1905 the two met there, where the father was working on road construction or in a quarry. He immediately fell in love with this pretty girl, not yet seventeen, and married her in spite of the fact that she was already the mother of a boy of six months. Wieser was born on April 30, 1906, the first of their three children. The father, constantly searching for jobs paying higher wages, took his family to several German cities. Early in 1913 he got work in a gigantic mine in Lintfort, an industrial town close to the Ruhr district. However, after two years there, Wieser's father had to join the Austrian army, and the family was ordered to move to his birth-place, Lohnsburg in Austria. In the neighboring village of Waldzell one of the father's sisters gave the family—the mother and four children—a home, consisting of only one room.

Because of the father's inadequate salary, the children had never had enough clothes and were able to wear shoes only in winter. None of their apartments in any of the German cities where they lived had had a bathroom; none of the children had ever received a present, either at Christmas or on birthdays, and the family did not own a single book. But they had had enough to eat.

"Life began to be really hard for us after we settled in Waldzell, when I was just ten years old," Wieser told me. "It was especially bad after March 1917, when our father died. He was wounded in a tunnel the Austrian soldiers were digging through a mountain on the border of Italy when their dynamite exploded too soon and trapped them; then he literally starved to death in a hospital in Linz. For several years after that there were days when we had almost noth-ing at all to eat. We often had to beg for scraps of food."

Wieser paused in his narrative, perhaps thinking I had heard enough for one evening. I could not let him stop but begged him to go on.

"For two years following February 1919 I was employed by one of the largest and richest peasants in Waldzell and received more and better food than I had ever had in my life," Wieser continued. "But the price I had to pay was a life almost like a slave's." In summer he had to get up at four A.M., work all day in the barns and fields, and then work in the kitchen until ten at night.

In winter he did not have to get up until six. In addition to having to work such long days, this small weak boy was expected to do the heavy work of a grown man. "What I minded even more," Wieser continued, "was that, although my greatest wish was to learn, I had to stop going to Wald-zell's little elementary school before I was thirteen. And now Sundays were also workdays for me, except for an hour in church—we were Roman Catholics—so I could no longer meet and play with the friends I had made in school. I missed the friendliness and approval of my teacher and some of the children in school, and of the priest, the sacristan, and many people in church. I had been an acolyte, and I never missed a service or made mistakes in the course of my duties.

"These were years of misery, but I was comforted by my deep religious belief. No matter how unhappy I was, I always hoped that God, because of my passionate belief in His power and goodness, would sometime reward me with a better life."

"And did He?" I asked.

"A great change in my life did occur shortly before I turned fifteen," replied Wieser. "I was able to leave Waldzell and the farm. With the help of one of my father's brothers, my older half-brother Tony and I found work in a glass factory in Schneegattern, some ten miles from Waldzell. The contrast to Waldzell was wonderful. I was no longer the lowest of the low but was socially the equal of the six hundred people employed in the factory. And I really began to study. I joined all the cultural organizations of the Socialist movement and the trade unions and almost every evening I attended some lecture or other. I read a great many of the books in the local library run by the Social Democrats. At age fifteen I read a book—the first in my life—*The Origins of the Family, of Private Property and the State,* by Friedrich Engels."

Within a year after his arrival in Schneegattern Wieser was elected chairman of the Socialist Youth group, and a year later he delivered to its members his first lecture, entitled "The Development of Human Exploitation from the Slavery of Antiquity to Present-day Capitalism." Because of his long working days in Waldzell he had never been able to get enough sleep. But in Schneegattern, he told me, he slept even less in spite of the eight-hour workday. His passionate longing for more knowledge led him to read several hours after the evening activities of the Socialist organizations.

"For the first time in my life I was truly happy," Wieser continued. "I no longer depended on the comfort of religion. This need was gradually replaced by a passion for a world of freedom and equality among all social groups and for lasting peace among all nations."

"What happened after that?" I asked.

"After five years in Schneegattern I spent eight years, between September 1926 and spring 1934, in St. Veit an der Glan in Carinthia. Thanks to all I had learned in Schneegattern, especially after I was laid off early in 1925 and was free to study all day, I was offered the job of leader of St. Veit's Socialist Youth and director of its Socialist Children's Education and Recreation Center. For four years I would study in my free hours and on my free days and learned even more through all my professional activities. At the end of those four years," Wieser continued with a laugh, "I wrote a series of lectures for my older pupils—three hundred pages containing everything I knew, with the all-embracing title: 'From the Origin of the Universe to the Society of the Future.' "

As Secretary of the Social Democratic party for the Carinthian district of St. Veit, Wieser had plenty of time to study. Some time after the establishment of the Austrian Fascist dictatorship in February 1934, he was imprisoned for four months because of his anti-Fascist underground work and then expelled from Carinthia.

"I decided to go to Vienna in August 1934," Wieser said with a smile, "to continue my illegal political activity. So here I am."

I was deeply moved by all that Wieser had told me, but was even more so when, after relating this story of hardship and suffering, he said with complete sincerity, "You see, I have always been lucky. Everything always turns out well for me."

We must have talked until midnight. Then, like good Austrians, we shook hands good night.

I had arranged for Herr Winter, formerly the Socialist mayor of the little village of Sulz who now often helped me at the cottage, to come up the next morning with a load of wood and some supplies. I wanted him to see me and my guest together. I told him that Wieser would be staying for a week or so and that I would be going back and forth. Herr Winter was used to my having guests of various nationalities, singly or in groups, with me or without me, and nothing could have been more natural. I had intended to leave Sulz that evening but decided there was an errand I ought to do at once. Wieser had only the clothes he was wearing when he left his room after the visit from the police: a pair of black striped trousers and a tight-fitting brown jacket, obviously city clothes and in any case too small. for him. They were inappropriate and conspicuous in the country. I left in the afternoon and went to a big store for men on the Mariahilferstrasse. Never having bought a man's suit before, I was quite embarrassed. I thought it would seem strange to the salesman that the man for whom the suit was intended did not come in himself, so I told him that I was looking for a knickerbocker suit for my fourteen-year-old son, who was away at school, and gave him the approximate size. The salesman was most helpful, and I soon selected a dark-green tweed suit, a sweater, and long wool socks. I took them out to Wieser the next evening and was delighted to find that they fit and that he liked them. (This suit survived many vicissitudes. Finally Wieser wore it—the warmest thing he had—when he was interned in a French camp during the cold, rainy autumn of 1939.)

The day Wieser was to leave Sulz, I returned to close up the cottage. He had grown a mustache, something I never got used to and never really liked. It did change his appearance considerably and, as he now wore a hat for the first time in his life, he felt it unlikely that he would be recog-

nized on the street. Wieser's plan was to sleep at the apartments of various friends one night at a time, with no fixed
lodging. I offered my apartment in the Lammgasse, and he
did in fact sleep there several nights during the next weeks.

One night in March Wieser went to Hermann's to sleep
but, approaching the door, saw someone he suspected of
being a police agent. He came to the Lammgasse instead
and indeed the next day learned that the police had been at
Hermann's. From then on, for three full years, my workroom was to be Wieser's home. We decided that I should
break off contact with all my other political friends, to lessen
the danger to them, to Wieser, and to myself. It was hard
for me to do this. I knew they would feel that I was a coward,
that I was letting them down. I was able to reason myself
out of this conflict by accepting that such a break was absolutely necessary for all concerned and that my discomfort
in doing so was a matter of vanity rather than good sense.
I told my political friends that I needed more time for my
studies and my child.

It was at about this time that Wieser—whom I shall here-
after call Joe—and I became lovers. It happened very naturally, perhaps inevitably, the night he returned to Vienna
after a dangerous trip to Czechoslovakia. Our love as well
as our liking for each other had been growing since our first
evening at Sulz; now suddenly we recognized it. I was immensely happy except for one thing—parting with Stephen.
Nothing had happened to make me care less for him, but
someone had entered my life whom I loved more. It was
painful for me and would surely be equally so for Stephen.
I wrote him a long letter, explaining as best I could what
had happened and hoping that he and I could remain friends.
And indeed we have been the best of friends ever since.

Formerly I had studied in my workroom many evenings
and returned home to sleep. Now I sometimes slept in the
Lammgasse apartment; I would get up at five-thirty to buy
fresh rolls and milk and the newspaper for Joe and to make
sure there was no one watching the apartment. I would leave

at six-thirty for a seven o'clock pathology course, which was always crowded a half-hour before it began, and then go home at eight for breakfast with Connie and Gerda. I attended few other classes, except for the labs. It was the custom to take cram courses, one at a time, in preparation for each examination. Each course took about an hour a day for a few weeks, and one studied that single subject furiously during that period. Harold Harvey and I often met for an hour in my apartment or in a café to test each other.

I was still going to my analysis five hours a week (down from six or seven), and now I had another task to fit in two or three times weekly: delivering messages between Joe and Lore, my only contact with our comrades. Lore worked in a lending library, and the messages were concealed in the books I took out or returned. Lore would pass Joe's messages on to designated comrades and make appointments for Joe, of which she would inform him in the books I picked up. Joe had by this time become chairman of the Central Committee of the entire Austrian underground Socialist party, now called the Revolutionary Socialists. He therefore, besides keeping in close touch with the comrades in Austria, had considerable correspondence with Otto Bauer and had to do much writing of his own. Lore served as Joe's secretary, meeting with him when necessary on a weekend or evening in her apartment to take dictation, sometimes writing secret messages to Bauer in invisible ink between the typed lines of some harmless personal letter, which she then sent to a cover address in Brno.

I still managed to have breakfast and lunch with Connie and usually spent a couple of hours with her in the late afternoon, playing with her, giving her supper, putting her to bed, and reading to her. On Gerda's day off Connie and I did something pleasant together—in fine weather it was usually an outing in the Vienna Woods. I saw my English friends occasionally and a few Austrian friends, particularly Franz Urbach, who had tutored me in physics, and his wife, Annie, daughter of the analyst Paul Federn. I could not possibly have led such a full life—although I might have learned more medicine—had I been attending an American medical school.

Joe seldom came to the Rummelhardtgasse but was often with us in Sulz for the weekend. He was known to Connie and Gerda as "Herr Josef": neither of them ever asked his full name or where he lived. In fact Connie, who was otherwise so full of curiosity, showed an extraordinary tact in this situation, never embarrassing us during the three years Joe was in hiding. Once, when Connie was perhaps five, Joe was lunching with us in our apartment, a rare occurrence. Unexpectedly the doorbell rang. Without a word, Joe picked up his place mat, plate, and glass and went into the next room. At the door I found one of Connie's playmates and her mother and invited them in, with some trepidation. Connie greeted them perfectly naturally and said not a word about Herr Josef.

I worried a great deal as to what to tell Connie about Joe and concluded that I should not say anything about our illegal work. If she should ever be questioned by the police, or even by friends or acquaintances, it would be best for her to know nothing at all. I did not want to tell her: "Don't ever say anything about this." I did not like being so secretive, but Connie's tact and discretion made it unnecessary for me ever to have to lie to her. I had confidence that—whatever she suspected—she would handle it well, and she always did. Only when both she and Joe were safely out of Austria after the Anschluss in March 1938 did Connie's questions pour out, and we were happy to be able to answer them.

In March 1935 I failed my histology examination. This was not a catastrophe, since one was allowed to repeat an exam up to four times, but it was necessary to take the physiology exam before repeating histology. I never understood the reason—if there was one—for this strange rule. It was a nuisance, but I passed the physiology and took histology again on April 30. It is easy to remember the date, as it is Joe's birthday. Joe was hiding in Sulz, since it was best to be especially careful over May Day. To my great relief, I passed the examination; then I took the bus to the cottage, where Joe had made garlands of fresh green leaves to twine about the fireplace and had decked the house with primroses, violets, cowslips, and other lovely wildflowers in every available vase or mug. I unpacked the dinner I had brought and my presents—a book, a shirt, and a tie—and we spent a wonderfully happy evening in the cozy little house. The next morning—May Day—grass and wildflowers were covered with an inch or more of snow.

Joe and I were planning our first vacation together for June or July. I wanted to visit my mother, who was in London with my stepfather, Francis Neilson, formerly a member of the British parliament. Joe would spend a week in Brussels and then meet me in London. Connie and Gerda were going to the Wörthersee in southern Austria with Connie's good friend Hanne Deutsch and Hanne's parents. Our friend Berta Bornstein was to be there also.

Joe left for Czechoslovakia a few days before I left Vienna. We met in a third-class railway carriage in Prague and traveled on together to Brussels, where Joe was to meet with Friedrich Adler, chairman of the Second (or Socialist) International. Joe had been furnished with a Czech passport with his photograph, in the name of Dr. Ernst Janisch, a Czech citizen. I stayed just one full day with him in Brussels, where we visited some great fair or exposition. My only vivid recollection of that day is of riding on the roller coasters and the exhilarating feeling of being really carefree after so many months of tension.

I stayed with my mother and stepfather in London at the Savoy Hotel for about a week, during which I had to look for a place where Joe and I could stay without his being in any way conspicuous. I found a large, busy hotel where I could rent a housekeeping apartment for a long or short period in my name without reporting who else would be staying there. It was ideal. The public rooms, halls, and stairways were always so crowded that there was no likelihood of anyone's being noticed. It was a little awkward explaining to my mother the real reason I was moving to a different hotel in London. I told her I wanted to see friends who hadn't the right clothes to appear at the Savoy and would not feel comfortable meeting me there. This was in fact true, although not the principal reason. Mother was used to my threadbare friends and also to my preference for less elegant and less expensive places than the Savoy. Appropriate dress was very important to my mother, and she accepted this explanation. I still saw her frequently and once took her to my apartment, having first carefully locked up Joe's meager wardrobe. I had told him what time we would be arriving, and he was in the lobby to catch a glimpse of mother without her having the slightest idea.

It never bothered my conscience to deceive my mother in these matters. Anything else would have been impossible. I am not referring now to Joe's illegal status—simply to mother's attitude toward any man in my life who was not my husband. I suppose this is not surprising for one of her generation, but I used to wonder about it. From my college days on, I had been convinced that a marriage certificate was unimportant—except to conform to our legal standards and protect children from the disadvantage of being illegitimate. I simply could not understand the horror people felt for an intimate relationship without marriage. It is a great satisfaction to me now, more than forty years later, that many people are beginning to share the views I have held most of my life.

I saw several old friends in London and for the first time met Joe's brother Loisl. Joe and I enjoyed going out to restaurants, theaters, and public places together, pleasures we had had to avoid in Vienna. It was a joy just to ride on a bus together or visit a museum.

After London Joe and I spent a week in Brittany, at a small hotel near the tiny village of Ploumanach. It was the best part of our vacation. Every day we took our bathing clothes, books, and a picnic lunch (including cold lobster, an every-day dish even at the simplest inn in this fishing village) and walked over the heath to the huge, smooth rocks which remained above sea level even when the great tides came in. It was a week of sunshine and quiet and joy.

Following our stay in Brittany, Joe remained in Paris and I traveled to Wörthersee to get Connie and take her for a few weeks to the shore of the Adriatic. This too was a lovely vacation; we both loved swimming and boating and playing in the sand. But before our vacation ended I received news of a terribly sad occurrence: Hertha had committed suicide by hanging herself.

I have often asked myself whether I should have foreseen this tragedy. I knew Hertha was unhappy and often de-pressed, but at that time I had little psychiatric knowledge of depression or suicide. Several times I myself had been tempted by suicide, but only in acute situations of loss or conflict. Had Hertha been experiencing some great loss— loss of a person, loss of love, of an ideal or of a hope? I had sometimes suspected that she was in love with Cornelius, although she spoke of him with sober objectivity. If she had indeed been in love with him, had she concluded that her love was hopeless? Did her mixed feelings produce in her an unbearable, unsolvable conflict? Or was Hertha in a chronic state of unhappiness, which increased gradually to the breaking point, with no specific precipitating cause? Possibly Isa Strasser might have been able to throw more light on this, but I was too shy to ask her. I shall never know.

My life with Joe continued in much the same way during the next two years. At some point I was able to improve the living quarters in the Rummelhardtgasse by renting the two-room apartment next to ours and having a door cut through.

I now had my own bedroom, a real luxury after having bunked
in the living-dining room, and my own bath. There was an
extra room where I could comfortably put up one or two
guests. A number of American and English friends did visit
me during these years, and—now that the apartment had
two separate entrances—Joe occasionally joined us.

We always had to consider what Joe would do if the police
should come. Before the apartment was enlarged he had
counted on jumping out the back window, only one story
above the alleyway. Now, he might be able to escape through
the second entrance door. I should mention that the entrance doors in Vienna had little peepholes which one could—
and of course did—peer out of, to see who was there before
opening the door. Nevertheless, Joe came rarely.

The new apartment gave Joe the opportunity to become
acquainted with Gladys Lack and with my archaeologist
friends Silva and Kirsopp Lake when they visited me. I had
explored archaeological sites in Palestine with Silva and Kirsopp, whom we called K, and had spent a month with them
at the monastery on Mt. Sinai—which at that time could be
reached only after riding a camel in the desert and mountains for three days—studying early Christian Greek manu-
scripts. All these friends Joe got to know better in Salzburg
in the summers of 1936 and 1937.

Salzburg was the only place in Austria where Joe and I
dared to appear together openly. It was so completely a tourist spot during the weeks of the music festival that we believed Joe would not be conspicuous in a party of Americans
and Britishers. Before we left Vienna I bought him grey flan-
nel trousers and a British-looking blazer, and we felt he was
well disguised.

Gerda left us to be married in the spring of 1936 and went
with her husband to Persia. We were very sad to lose her.
Another lovely young kindergarten teacher, Fini Wodak, came
to live with us. Connie, Fini, and I traveled to Salzburg together, and Joe joined us there after a few days in Czecho-

slovakia. I tried always to be in Vienna when Joe was there, so I traveled only when he had to be away. Besides Gladys, Silva and K, and other friends, Stephen and Tony were in Salzburg, and one of those summers Harold Harvey also was there. It was a new experience for Joe and me to be together with good friends, and we both enjoyed it greatly. Joe got on well with my friends, and in this carefree, congenial atmosphere we were all full of life and laughter. I remember, perhaps mistakenly, the weather as fine. I know we walked and swam and made excursions to the lakes and mountains. Every evening we would listen to superb music and after that we'd sit talking in a café or a wine cellar, often until late.

In January 1937 Joe and I first went to Arosa to ski. I thought I would prefer to spend our vacation in Italy or some southern spot, but Joe prevailed on me to try to ski. Except for a few easy runs on the slopes at Sulz, I had had little experience. Joe was a kind and thorough teacher and skiing has been a special joy to me ever since. Arosa was the loveliest mountain spot I had ever seen; the snow and weather were perfect; I learned how to climb comfortably and to ski down with ease, and I am eternally grateful to Joe for overcoming my resistance and taking me to the winter mountains.

In the spring of 1937 Connie, Fini, and I spent a week with my mother in Paris. My oldest brother, Nelson, was there also and was, in spite of his wife's protestations, to return with a friend to the United States on the zeppelin *Hindenburg*. Nelson had always been interested in and attracted by new technology, inventions, experiments, explorations, adventure, perhaps even danger. On our arrival in Vienna, after twenty or so hours on the train, I found a cable from Edward, my other brother: "Nelson definitely saved." This was, fortunately, the first news I had of the disaster at Lakehurst, New Jersey. When fire broke out aboard the ship, Nelson, imploring his friend to join him, jumped to safety.

His friend did not. Nelson made three attempts to go back into the ruins to save his friend, incurring severe burns of his hands and ears and a deep laceration of the leg. His friend perished with so many others.

The years 1936 and 1937 were, with a few changes, a continuation of the life I have described. I became more involved in my medical studies and really enjoyed much of the clinical work, not only in psychiatry but also in surgery, gynecology, and obstetrics. I had some excellent teachers, including Dr. Ludwig Adler, who had been my gynecologist and obstetrician.

I, like all medical students, was required to take an *Internat* in obstetrics, twice spending five or six days and nights in the General Hospital so as to be on hand for all the deliveries. This was my only "collegiate" experience during my medical training, since I had been too busy—and possibly considered myself too old (I was thirty-four)—to take part in the social or extracurricular activities of the other students, who were in their early twenties.

To my surprise, I enjoyed the *Internat* both times. About twelve of the women students bunked together in one dormitory, and at least that many men stayed in another dormitory. In the evening, when we were not attending the deliveries, we all got together for talking, singing, and sharing whatever snacks we had. Whenever the bell announcing an impending delivery sounded, we would all rush to the labor room to observe. Except for the birth of my own child, this was my first such experience and I became very interested in obstetrics. (Later, during my medical internship in America, I liked obstetrics best.) Since I lived only two or three minutes' walk from the hospital and could be called back to the hospital if a delivery was about to occur, I was able to arrange to go home a couple times a day to see Connie.

Analysts have often asked me whether I had had any conflict about telling Dr. Brunswick of my illegal activities. I don't believe I ever gave it a thought. She was, of course, an American; furthermore, I knew she shared my views. (Analysts were not as reticent in expressing their opinions at that time as they have since become—at least in the United States.) If I had ever suspected Dr. Brunswick of any Fascist tendencies, it certainly would have caused me conflict and I suppose I would have stopped my analysis.

My analysis was gradually coming to an end. In 1936 I began to see Dr. Brunswick less often, then, for a few months, only when I asked for an appointment, and finally, in late 1936 or early 1937, I believe, our sessions stopped altogether. It happened so naturally that I do not remember even discussing termination. My analyst and I were evidently in perfect accord about this, knowing it was happening and that it was right that it should. There was no solemn good-bye between us. I saw Dr. Brunswick occasionally for as long as she remained in Vienna, but these meetings were not analytic hours.

After completing the required ten semesters of medical school, I was eligible in the fall of 1937 to begin to take the eleven final examinations. Six of these constituted the so-called "second rigorosum" and the remaining five the "third rigorosum." All had to be taken in a certain sequence. If a student failed any examination, he or she had to take all the others of that rigorosum before repeating it.

I considered myself particularly well prepared for the first examination, pathology, having attended Professor Chiari's excellent early-morning lectures for a couple of years, performed an unusually large number of autopsies, and taken a cram course given by Chiari's assistant, Dr. Piringer. This cram course emphasized bacteriology, and we studied a few hundred slides. One advantage of the course was that we were told which of these slides—about half, I think—might be given us at the examination and which definitely would not. Dr. Piringer was an authority; it was said that his statements were completely reliable.

My first question at the examination was to identify a slide. I immediately went into a panic, since the slide appeared to me to be a sample of anthrax without spores, which Dr. Piringer had stated categorically would never be used in the examination. I tried and tried to think of something else that it could possibly be and finally, in desperation, decided on some other bacterium with certain resemblances, although I could not believe my answer was right. All the examinations were oral, which I disliked. I'll never forget Dr. Chiari's horrified look, after I had made the wrong identification, as he said to me simply: "Aber, Frau Doktor!" I had failed.

As I was leaving the building I saw Dr. Piringer. "Did you tell us anthrax without spores is never shown in the examination?" "It's never shown," he replied, with his friendly smile. Not feeling at all friendly, I told him he had just caused me to flunk. I was angry at him for giving me the wrong information but much more furious with myself for not trusting my own judgment. I had failed because I had acted stupidly. Now I would have to take five more examinations, at intervals, before I could repeat pathology, and I wanted to cry. However, with a busy day ahead of me, I forced myself to get through my tasks.

After supper I went to the Lammgasse apartment to wait for Joe, whom I expected at about eight o'clock, eager to tell him of my disappointment. He didn't come and he didn't call. At first I was irritated; then, as the hours passed, I became more and more worried. I was sure the police had got him. I have seldom been more miserable than I was that night. Finally, at one A.M., Joe called and I went down to the predetermined place to bring him up to the apartment. He simply had been delayed. Now I was angry that he had not found some way to let me know, and I cried all night.

In November 1937 Joe and I were jolted out of our routine by a series of events that struck us like a thunderbolt. Joe had to be in Brno for about a week, and I used this week to have a minor operation which would keep me in the hospital for a few days. The day I came out I went to the lending library to pick up messages from Lore. She was not there, so I returned a harmless book to one of the librarians and selected another. As this was the first time Lore had been absent, I was immediately alarmed. The following day, a Saturday, I telephoned the library and asked for Lore, of course using her real name. She was not there. When I asked whether she would be in on Monday, the brief answer was "I don't know."

The pleasure and relief I always felt at Joe's safe return were marred by our fears for Lore. On Sunday Joe went to the large apartment house where she lived, walked up the stairs past her apartment, and saw that her door mat had been taken in—the prearranged signal that she had been arrested. This same day, I believe, Joe learned of the arrest of several of his closest fellow workers; soon almost every one of them had been seized as part of a massive roundup of Socialists. It was the greatest piece of luck that Joe had been away at just this time—but we were quite unable to feel anything but the most painful distress.

Plans had to be made rapidly. I went to Brno to report all we knew to Otto Bauer and to work out various strategies with him. We all were agreed that Joe should not remain in Vienna, and he left soon for Brussels, from where he later went on to Switzerland. Much of our work in Vienna came to a standstill.

Connie, Fini, and I met Joe in Arosa, Switzerland, for Christmas. We stayed at an unusually attractive hotel, standing solitary on the ski slopes high above the village. It was Connie's first real skiing experience, and she took to it as a bird to the air. It was a joyful time in spite of Joe's and my worries. We were worried not just about our comrades, the setback in our work, and the increasingly desperate outlook for Austria, but also, more and more, about the state of the world. In Germany, Nazi power was growing, Nazi threats were increasing. In Spain, the war was heartbreaking. In America, the Depression was frightening. In Russia,

Stalin had long since destroyed early hopes that anything resembling socialism could ever be achieved there. Such fragile peace as existed in the world seemed at the point of death. But our sadness and fears could not annihilate the joy of skiing down the slopes in Arosa's life-giving sunshine.

Joe remained abroad while I returned to Vienna in early January 1938 to take a few more examinations and act as contact between him and comrades in Austria. Of the most active Viennese Socialists, only Joe's good friend Karl Holoubek and one other remained outside prison walls. However, they were in touch with a number of hitherto more obscure young Socialists who were now trying to mobilize forces to carry on at least a minimum of the work. Holoubek also had contact with friends in the provinces who had not been caught in the Vienna roundup.

A message had been sent in some roundabout way to Holoubek to meet me at the Sulz cottage the Sunday after my return. On Saturday afternoon I went out there alone for the weekend. I had met Holoubek a few times in the fall of 1934, had liked and trusted him, and was happy to see him again. This was the first of several meetings during which I passed on Joe's instructions, suggestions, and questions and Holoubek gave me all his information and questions to write to Joe. My letters to Joe, addressed to Dr. Ernst Janisch and written in English, contained this information disguised in medical and scientific terms. Joe and I had worked out a private code for certain names and important items, and it was fairly easy to make everything understood to each other. Our opponents, for instance, were "antibodies." If I wrote Joe about himself he was "Dr. Meadows," since his first cover-name, Wieser, sounded much like *Wiese,* meaning "meadow."

In early February, having passed my two examinations, I took another vacation, this time without Connie, and met Joe in Switzerland. From there we proceeded together to Paris, where I met Friedrich and Kathia Adler for the first time. Friedrich Adler, the son of Viktor Adler, who in 1866 had founded the Austrian Social Democratic party and became its first leader, was himself a leftist Socialist and a pacifist. In 1916, Friedrich Adler had publicly assassinated the dictatorial prime minister, Karl Stürgkh, as a protest against Stürgkh's support of war and his refusal in July 1914, when war was threatening, to convene parliament. Adler had been condemned to death but the sentence was commuted, and he was amnestied in 1918 when the Hapsburg Empire collapsed.

Whatever one might think of the assassination, one could not help recognizing Friedrich Adler as a man of integrity and courage. He seemed to me an essentially gentle man. I was impressed and also charmed by both Friedrich and his Russian-born wife, Kathia. Kathia and I immediately felt close to each other and remained friends as long as she lived. (Later, when I got to know their son, Felix, I liked him very much also.)

It was in Paris that Joe and I learned the portentous news of Schuschnigg's February 12 meeting with Hitler in Berchtesgaden, during which the Austrian chancellor had had to make many concessions to the Nazis. We looked at each other in consternation, convinced that it could now be only a matter of weeks until the Nazis would take Austria. We returned to Vienna on February 16 or 17. As one result of the Berchtesgaden meeting, Schuschnigg, obliged to grant amnesty to the Nazis, had amnestied all political prisoners, and we found our comrades at liberty on our return.

Vienna was seething with uncertainty and unrest, though not everyone was as convinced as Joe and I were that the Nazis would soon be in power. It had been decided that Joe would leave Austria immediately if this should come to pass. He set about trying to persuade those who would be most in danger to leave the country at once, or at least to get their passports and papers in order so that they might depart instantly when the Nazis took over. (Scarcely a one followed his adjurations.)

I did not believe myself to be in danger and intended to remain until I finished my medical course, probably in May. I was planning to take my next two examinations in the second half of March, before the university closed for the six-week spring vacation, and the last two exams when it reopened in May. Harold Harvey completed his examinations in early March and left immediately. I was sorry to see him go. He was the only colleague in medical school and the only American friend I had seen much of during these last four years.

Dr. Brunswick left Vienna about the same time, around March 8. Shortly before leaving she asked to see me, and we talked at length about the political situation, which we viewed in the same way. Dr. Brunswick was distressed that she had been unable to persuade the Freuds to leave Austria and begged me to do whatever I could to help them get away. She had already given affidavits of support to a number of friends to enable them to emigrate to the United States. This was, I believe, the first time I learned exactly what an affidavit was, and the first time I thought seriously about trying to get my Jewish friends to America. My concern up to this point had been chiefly to help our comrades get away to France, Switzerland, or some other feasible place.

The amnesty, and the implication that Schuschnigg might grant certain concessions to the Socialists because he now needed their support, made some of the Socialists optimistic and even rash. Joe tried desperately to make it clear that this was the most critical, the most dangerous period of all. The Berchtesgaden ultimatum had forced Schuschnigg to appoint the National Socialist Arthur Seyss-Inquart as Innenminister, the minister in charge of security, and to give him explicit control of the police. Joe immediately issued directives. The first, to the comrades who had been amnestied, sternly prohibited any political activity or contact with those who were continuing the illegal work. "The appointment of Seyss-Inquart," Joe wrote, "marks the birth of the Austrian Gestapo."

On March 9 Schuschnigg astounded the Austrian people by announcing that on Sunday, March 13, there would be a referendum for all Austrians to vote for or against a "free, independent Austria"—in essence to choose between Schuschnigg and Hitler.

Joe's tasks became still more urgent, and it was no longer possible to take the extreme precautions we were used to. We accumulated a certain amount of illegal literature—something that we had been careful not to do in less frantic times—which I kept in a locked closet in the Rummelhardt-gasse, hidden in a pile of harmless newspapers and magazines.

We were helped in those days by Tony Hyndman, who was visiting me. It was comforting to know we could rely on him. Joe sometimes asked him to deliver a message to a friend, and on March 11 Tony went out to the Sulz cottage to meet a comrade and exchange some important communications. Joe himself left early that morning for Brno, to confer with Otto Bauer. This fateful March 11 fell on a Friday, Fini's day off, and I was spending the day at home with Connie, who was recovering from a cold. I had put her to bed at about seven in the evening and was telling her a story, so I did not have the radio on when Schuschnigg made his memorable announcement: "I yield to force . . . God protect Austria."

Three

The Crowded Hour:
Vienna, from the Anschluss
to late June 1938

One crowded hour of glorious life
Is worth an age without a name.

—*Sir Walter Scott*

I had just settled Connie to sleep and was hurrying back to
the radio, to which I had been listening at intervals all day,
when the telephone rang. It was my dearest friend among
the analysts, Berta Bornstein, warning me as carefully and
as cryptically as she could to leave Vienna at once. She was
one of the few people who knew I was still deeply involved
in illegal activities, although she was not familiar with any
details. "I'm so worried about Connie's bronchitis," Berta
said. "I do hope you'll take her to the mountains right away.
You know the doctor said she really must have a change of
air." Not knowing that Austria had fallen to the Nazis only
minutes earlier, I protested that I didn't think it was that
urgent. "Oh, indeed it is," Berta said. "I'm so afraid she'll
get pneumonia if you don't leave soon."

Hastening to the radio in a corner room overlooking the
Spitalgasse, I heard unfamiliar sounds coming from the street.
Pulling back the curtains and opening the window, I looked

down at an unbelievable scene. The street had filled with
people, a solid, moving mass, many carrying swastika flags
and singing the Horst Wessel Lied—the Nazi song. What a
change had come about within half an hour! And I knew,
with a pounding heart, that what I saw was only a faint
harbinger of the profound changes about to disrupt all our
lives—only an intimation of future havoc, death, and destruction. This instantaneous vision of the future—perhaps
analogous to the panoramas of their pasts described by people faced with sudden death—made me faint and dizzy for
a moment. Then my head cleared.

My first thought was of Joe. He was presumably on the
train at this moment, returning from Czechoslovakia. If he
learned of the Nazi victory before reaching the Austrian
border he would have a chance to get off the train and return
to Brno. But I was not at all sure he would do so, knowing
he would be loath to leave our comrades without trying to
help them. And it was very likely that he was already in
Austria. He would certainly telephone me upon his arrival,
and I would tell him to come to the Rummelhardtgasse.

My next thought was to destroy the illegal literature we
had on hand. There was, unfortunately, no stove in which
I could burn the papers in this modern building—and no
fireplace, either. I began tearing them into small bits and
flushing them down the toilet. It was soon stopped up, but
the toilet continued its loud hissing. I feared this uninter-
rupted sound could be heard through the apartment's thin
walls, so I stood on a chair (the tank was high up) and was
finally able to stop the noise by forcing an inverted flower
pot under the lever. But the toilet no longer worked, and
since I did not dare risk clogging the other one, I once more
concealed the remaining papers.

Tony came in, reporting that the streets were so filled
with people that cars and trams were slowed and even walking was difficult. Shortly afterward, Joe called from a nearby
public phone and then came up. He had already decided to
seek out his most endangered comrades, urge them to leave,

and tell those who could not yet leave how to contact me. He asked me whether I had any money.

I had only a small account in an Austrian bank but kept a larger amount in a bank in Holland, which periodically sent me money, delivered to me personally in cash by the *Geldbriefträger*, literally the "money-mailman." Some days earlier, foreseeing a probable emergency, I had instructed the Dutch bank to send me a large amount of Austrian and also American money, in denominations of ten and twenty dollars. The "money-mailman" had come that very morning! I was thankful now, not only that I had the money, but also that my parents had impressed upon me from an early age the importance of always keeping enough money at hand for an emergency. The Austrian banks, closed for the weekend, remained closed for a number of days longer, and stringent currency regulations were put into effect. One serious problem for all who wished to leave the country was that one could use Austrian money for tickets only as far as the border, beyond which one had to pay the fare in foreign currency, which was not available! I don't remember now whether Austria prohibited taking Austrian money out of the country or whether other countries would not accept it for exchange. I rather think both; in any case the schilling was useless outside Austria. On that Friday evening I did not yet know all the complications, which were increasing hourly, but I rightly suspected that the American dollars would prove a lifesaver to some of our friends and was more than happy to give them to Joe to deliver. He and Tony set out together.

Joe had repaired the toilet, so I resumed my task of destroying papers, tearing them into even smaller bits or burning them one by one over the toilet. I would pause every few minutes to listen to the radio or occasionally to receive a cautious telephone call from some worried friend. Meanwhile I was thinking out our immediate plans. When I had asked Joe, during the few minutes he had been at the apartment, whether he would leave on the morning train for Switzerland, he had not replied directly but had given me the impression he did not want to do so. "Remember that it was decided by both of us and by all your friends that you *must* leave at once," I said. He went out without committing himself.

After a while I turned off the radio, so as to concentrate on the question of what would be best for Connie. Until now I had not seriously thought of sending her out of Austria before I myself could leave. Berta's call, although possibly intended primarily as a warning to me, made me reconsider the danger to Connie if she remained. I realized that I could no longer be as careful as I had been; there would be a much higher chance of my being arrested. And if I were detained, whatever the outcome, it would be hard on Connie. In any case, I would be busier and under greater stress than ever before; it would not be a good life for her. As for myself, I would feel more relaxed, more free to do whatever was necessary, if I knew that Connie was safe.

There was yet another reason to send Connie abroad. We had invited Pups, the son of our friends Silva and K Lake, to spend six months with us in Vienna while his parents went to Turkey on an archaeological expedition. They were undoubtedly all on the *Queen Mary* on their way to France at this very moment. I knew I must prevent Pups from coming to Vienna. I decided to send Connie and Fini to Arosa and to arrange for Pups to join them there.

When I came to this decision, after just a few minutes' hard thinking, I felt immensely relieved. I was certain that it was the right thing to do. (Later, when I found how busy I was every day from morning to late in the night and how much danger I was inevitably exposed to, I wondered that I had ever considered keeping Connie with me.) I wanted Connie, Fini, and Joe to go to Switzerland together the next morning and thought it would be a good idea if Tony accompanied them. Tony and Connie both had British passports, which would give Joe some protection. Fini came home sometime during the evening but I said nothing to her about my plan, since Joe had not yet consented.

Joe and Tony returned about midnight, bringing with them Peperl and Hilde Bohmer, old Socialist friends of Joe's, who were, however, politically inactive as well as obviously Aryan and therefore were in a good position to help in this zero hour. I had never met them. They stayed only long enough for us to agree on some story as to how we had met, arrange how to contact each other in the future, and decide on a few code words and signals. Then all four departed.

It was probably two or three in the morning when Joe and Tony came back again, this time with Holoubek and his wife. We made arrangements for me to get their photographs and take them to Brno to be substituted for photographs in the passports of some Czech comrades whose descriptions would approximately apply to them. When the Holoubeks had left, Joe told me of his largely unsuccessful attempts to see our comrades. Hardly anyone had been home, but in some cases Joe had left a message cautiously indicating where and when I could be reached. He now gave me directions to the house of "Little" Otto Bauer and told me when to meet and how to recognize Pav, a comrade I did not know, at a certain café and how to contact several others.

When I told Joe and Tony of my conviction that they, Connie, and Fini should travel together to Switzerland, Tony immediately agreed but Joe said he had to give it more thought. I promised to wake Tony early in any case, and he went to bed for the few remaining night hours while Joe and I continued talking, planning what was most important for me to do and how I was to go about it. By five o'clock Joe had agreed to take the morning train to Switzerland; they would all have to leave the apartment at about seven.

I awakened Connie and asked her, "How would you like to go back to Arosa with Fini for a while? You know Dr. Bien thought a change of air would do you good." Connie, overjoyed, jumped out of bed and began to dress. Next I

Portrait of the author as a Wellesley undergraduate

The burning of the Palace of Justice in Vienna, July 1927 (*Dokumentationsarchiv des österreichischen Widerstandes*)

Fighting in front of the Arbeiterheim (Workers' Center) in a district of Vienna, February 1934 (*Dokumentationsarchiv des österreichischen Widerstandes*)

A photo of the author taken in 1934 by Trude Fleischmann

Joe Buttinger at the typewriter in Paris, 1939

A portrait of Joe in the early 1950s

Connie at age six, shortly before the Anschluss

Nine-year-old Connie and Klecks in Pennington, 1940

Nazi students demonstrating in front of Vienna University, February 1938, after Schuschnigg agreed to amnesty Nazi party members at his Berchtesgaden meeting with Hitler (*Dokumentationsarchiv des österreichischen Widerstandes*)

Nazis changing street names in Vienna, March 1938 (*Dokumentationsarchiv des österreichischen Widerstandes*)

The cottage at Sulz in the Vienna Woods

A marble bust of the author made by
the sculptor S. T. Konenkov in New
York, 1926

awakened Fini and asked her to pack for herself and Connie;
then I took Connie and her little dog, Klecks, out to the
shop around the corner to buy fresh rolls, butter, and milk
for breakfast.

Stepping out on the street, we saw an enormous swastika
flag flying over the General Hospital across the street. I told
Connie as succinctly as I could what had happened. She was
well informed politically and immediately grasped the essentials. I said Joe and Tony would travel with her and Fini
as far as Sargans in Switzerland, the town where they would
have to change trains for Arosa; but I left it to Joe to explain
as much as he thought wise about the reasons for his leaving
Austria. I myself suspected that Connie already had a very
good idea of what these were. (Joe later told me that he had
given Connie a brief explanation of his underground work
and had told her that he was well known in the provinces
through which the train would pass and might be recognized
or suspected by some official checking the passengers. He
had begun to tell her what she should or should not say if
anyone questioned her about him when Connie interrupted:
"Wouldn't it be better if I just pretended I don't understand
German?" "Much better," Joe agreed.)

I gave Joe a small suitcase in which to put his toilet articles—the only possessions he had with him—and a few of
Tony's things. Connie wore her ski suit and as usual carried
one or two of her beloved toy animals. All had English books
and magazines and—with three pairs of skis—looked, as they
started off for the station, like a jolly party of vacationers.

Immediately after seeing them into a taxi, I too left the
apartment, conscious of the urgency of my tasks. Having
taken a tram to the neighborhood of "Little" Otto Bauer's
home, I walked past the house to make sure no one was
watching and on to the nearest shop, where I purchased a
pack of cigarettes; then I returned to the house. I met Otto's
wife, Rosa, for the first time. The Bauers' four children were
between nine and sixteen years of age. The parents believed
that Poldi and Rosi, the two older girls, could visit Austrian

friends near the Swiss border, get a tourist pass for a day's bus trip into Switzerland, and simply leave the bus there. Swiss comrades, good friends of the Bauers, would meet them and take them to their home in Zurich. I got descriptions of Otto and Rosa and the two younger children, arranged to get their photographs on Monday, and left money with them.

I continued such meetings throughout the morning, returning at about one o'clock. We had left the apartment in great disorder early that morning, before Frau Kathe, our housekeeper, had arrived. When I unlocked the door Frau Kathe burst into tears of joy. "I thought you had all left, all fled," she wept. She was obviously unhappy about the Nazi takeover, but we both realized it would be better not to say too much. I told her that I had sent Connie and Fini to Arosa and that Herr Josef and Herr Tony had gone also, but that Herr Tony would return in a few days.

After lunch I made my way to the Urbachs', through the ever-increasing number of German troops, cars, and tanks and below the circling airplanes. The noise of the low-flying planes together with the blaring of loudspeakers on the streets was deafening. Of all my politically inactive friends, the Urbachs were most on my mind. Knowing that Franz was engaged in important research in physics, I thought it imperative for them to leave the country immediately. I found them at home listening to the radio and periodically looking out the window at the astonishing transformation of their hitherto peaceful street. We embraced each other, hardly able to speak. Then I said: "You must go to America at once. I'm going to write you an affidavit of support. Have you got a typewriter?" We talked at length. I found Franz even more cautious and fearful than I had expected him to be. He was one of the early researchers of infrared-sensitive phosphors, which were not then perfected or known to the public but considered of military importance and therefore regarded by the Nazis as "top secret." Franz was almost as frightened about making any attempt to leave as he was about staying, but I persuaded him that it could do no harm to apply at once for a visa to the United States.

At this time no special forms were required to provide an affidavit; a simple letter and proof of support were sufficient. I suppose that as proof of support with this and the other affidavits I gave during these days I must have said that a statement from my bank would follow. I don't remember quite what I did to handle this most expediently. Perhaps I got a whole supply of letters from the bank at one time.

During these first days I found time to give affidavits to Berta Bornstein and Auge and soon afterwards to the psychoanalyst Anya Männchen and her husband, a Socialist and historian. To another analyst, Anny Katan, whom I had first known as Anny Angel, I gave an affidavit for her divorced husband and their son, Klaus Angel.

On Saturday, the day after the Anschluss, I returned home late in the afternoon from my visit with the Urbachs and found Sheila Grant-Duff in my apartment. Sheila, a young English friend whom I had first met in Vienna and who had been with me in Russia in 1932, was now a reporter in Prague. She had come to Vienna to witness the Anschluss firsthand. It was a comfort to talk with someone who would not be endangered by hearing my story. And it was a special bonus to have her with me that interminable evening as I waited for word that Joe was out of danger. I had been hoping for a call from Tony about eight o'clock, thinking that he would leave the train as soon as they had safely crossed the border. No call came at eight or at nine. By ten I was uneasy, by eleven really alarmed, by midnight almost in despair. Sheila's presence and being able to talk with her helped me to control my fears. At last, at about twelve-thirty, the telephone rang. Tony had remained on the train as far as Sargans, where he had accompanied Connie and Fini to a hotel for the night, and said he would put them on the train for Arosa the next day. Joe had continued on to Paris. At last I could let the tears come, tears not of despair but of thankful relief.

On Sunday afternoon Ania Herzog, a translator and editor whom I had known for several years, came to my apartment. She was undecided about whether she should leave Austria. We listened to the radio, talked, and were even able to laugh— a blessing during those anxious days. I persuaded her to go to Paris. Before Ania left Vienna, she sent Hermann Broch, the writer whom she had been helping with his work, to ask my advice about how he could cross the border. For a week or more Broch telephoned me frequently, with coded but nevertheless indiscreet questions, usually relating to a lost umbrella, which I could not figure out and which caused me great uneasiness. Broch finally did leave Austria and somehow got to Holland or Belgium. Later, when he was living in Princeton, I knew him well.

On Sunday evening, when I was again alone, my doorbell rang. Peering through the peephole I saw three figures—a man, woman, and child—standing before my door. Just a glance showed me that they were timid and worried and in need of help, so I unlatched the door and beckoned them in. "Mary," whispered the man, removing his hat and holding out his hand. "Hubert sent a message that I was to come to you." (Hubert was Joe's current cover-name.) "I'm Manfred Ackermann." I had not recognized him. From the once or twice I had seen him, in late 1934, I had gotten the impression of an active, youngish man with thick black hair. Now I saw a little, elderly man with a bald head. He had had his head completely shaved, and the transformation was spectacular.

Ackermann, still whispering, introduced me to his wife and nine-year-old son. He asked whether it was true that I could get him a false passport and whether I knew any place where he could hide until he got it. He was extremely anxious, as indeed he had every reason to be. Joe had indicated to me that Ackermann, a Jew and a Socialist leader, was in more danger than any of our other comrades and that he

should be the first to have help. It was difficult to converse
with him. He could not easily hear me because he was slightly
deaf, and I often could not hear him because he whispered.
Of course we did not want to shout; sometimes we even
wrote our questions or answers on scraps of paper. The Ack-
ermanns gave me their photographs and I told them I would
go to Brno on Monday afternoon after collecting photographs from other comrades. I hoped I could get a passport
for Ackermann promptly, since I was sure that the Brno
people were alerted to the urgency of his case and knew his
description; they were waiting only for my arrival with the
photograph. His wife and child were prepared to wait at
home.

I told Ackermann about my workroom in the Lammgasse,
but it was hard to convince him that it would be a safe place.
At last, since he had no alternative, he let me take him
there. His wife and son came along; in case we were observed by the concierge, it might look more innocent for us
to be four persons. Again I was thankful for this ideal setup
in the Lammgasse, one of the few buildings in Vienna where
the concierge's apartment was in the rear! We got into the
entrance hall, then into the elevator and out at my top-floor
studio without being seen by a soul. I think this was comforting to Mrs. Ackermann; nothing, unfortunately, could
reassure her poor husband. I learned later that Ackermann
was suffering from severe toothache, a condition that undoubtedly increased his anxiety. We pulled down the shades
and in whispers exchanged all the necessary information; I
made sure that there was adequate food, although Ackermann claimed he could not eat, and I showed him whatever
he needed to know about the kitchen and the studio; then,
promising to see him Tuesday afternoon, I left, accompanied
by his wife and child, who bade him a brave and loving
farewell.

We had decided together that it would be best for Ackermann to travel to Venice, in the belief that he would
undergo the least risk at the Italian border. Indeed, Switzer-

land and Italy were the only possibilities. As early as the
Friday night of Schuschnigg's abdication the first trainload
of refugees had been turned back at the Czech border. Ackermann was rightly reluctant to board the train at the Vienna station, which would surely be closely guarded by Nazi
police. It would be safer to board at Wiener Neustadt, a stop
about an hour from Vienna on the way south. I thought
Peperl Bohmer could be of help in this situation, since he
was an Aryan and had a car. Ackermann, who knew Peperl,
readily agreed. On my way home I called Peperl from a pay
station to alert him to our probable need of his help Tuesday
night.

On Monday I went to various agreed-upon rendezvous to
get photographs of a number of our comrades. Then I bought
myself a corset—the only one I ever wore in my life—to
conceal the false passports I intended to tape to my body.
In mid afternoon I took a train to Brno. I was already thankful that Connie was in Arosa and also that the university
had closed indefinitely; I was the sole mistress of my time.

The trip to Brno and back was mercifully uneventful. I
spent the evening with Otto Bauer and early the next morning was given a suitable Czech passport, with its original
photograph exchanged for Ackermann's and the stamps and
seals properly faked. I had left the photographs of our other
comrades with Bauer and agreed to return within a week for
as many passports as could be completed in that time.

Back in Vienna, I took the usual precautions as well as
some extra ones to make sure I was not being followed before making my way to the Lammgasse. I was pleased that
I had succeeded in obtaining the passport and that Ackermann would be able to leave that evening.

When I unlocked the door, however, I found the studio
empty! Nor was Ackermann in the kitchen, bedroom, or
bathroom. My first feeling was of disbelief; it seemed impossible that he could have vanished. I looked under the bed
and unlocked the tiny cupboard (which contained Joe's few
extra clothes and my volumes of Marx and Lenin), knowing

full well that no one could have squeezed in, even if he had found the well-hidden key. I then began searching for a note or a clue, looking under the cushions, under the rug, in the coffee canister, in every possible and impossible place. Finally I was forced to believe that my guest had really vanished without a trace.

The police must have come for him, I thought. But why had they not waited for me? Were they even now at the Rummelhardtgasse? What should I do with the precious passport, still taped to my body under the corset? There was no good place to hide it in the studio, and if the police had already been here, they would undoubtedly be back again to make a thorough search. On the other hand, if they were at the Rummelhardtgasse, my doom would be sealed if I did not get rid of the passport before going there. I decided to telephone, hoping that Frau Kathe could give me some hint.

To my relief, the phone was answered by Tony, who had returned the evening before. His cheerful voice was instantly reassuring. Nevertheless, I asked him to check our supplies in the kitchen and make a list of things I should shop for before returning home and told him I would call him again. This was our signal for him to go out and make sure no one was watching the house. When I called again fifteen minutes later, Tony gave me the sign that the coast was clear.

I was very glad Tony was back, and his news was comforting: there had been no telephone calls, no visitors, nor any unusual occurrences. Still, nothing he told me was able to clear up the mystery of the vanished guest. I hid the passport in the best place I could think of and waited.

An hour or so later an unknown voice called, giving a password to let me know he was a comrade. He then said casually that he was in the neighborhood and would like to drop in. I said, "Come up and have some coffee with me."

The tall, blond man who arrived in a few minutes greeted me as an old friend and called me Mary, even though I had never seen him before. I was by principle cautious at first,

but the stranger, who gave his name as Robert, quickly dispelled any possible suspicions. "I've just heard that Hubert
got safely to Paris," he told me with obvious pleasure. I
replied with the good news I had learned in Brno that "Hansi,"
Joe's former secretary, had also made it. "I know," he said
with a grin. "She's my sister."

Robert and his old friend Ackermann had somehow com-
municated—perhaps through Frau Ackermann; I am not clear
about the details—and Robert had gone to the Lammgasse.
One or both of them had thought it better for Ackermann
to go to a new, possibly safer hideout, and Robert had accompanied Ackermann there. Robert now gave me back the
duplicate keys I had left in the studio.

I told him that Peperl had agreed to drive Ackermann to
the Wiener Neustadt station that evening, where he could
board the night train for Venice. Robert said he would go
along to buy the ticket for Ackermann at the station's book-
ing office, a possible danger spot. He would also get himself
a ticket to someplace near the Austrian border, in order to
see Ackermann through the ordeal of having his ticket
checked by the conductor and to be with his friend as long
as possible. I promised to arrange with Peperl to pick the
two comrades up on a certain convenient street corner at
exactly nine o'clock—or whatever the appointed hour was.
We synchronized our watches to the second. I now handed
over to Robert the crucial passport, feeling as though I had
got rid of a burning coal. We shook hands and I wished him
"Hals und Beinbruch," the fanciful German equivalent of
"good luck."

When Peperl later came to my apartment to receive the
exact instructions, he persuaded me to accompany him in
the car. That way he could, if he were stopped by the police
at any point—such spot-checks were common in those days—
give a more plausible reason for being out on an evening's
drive: that he and I were "joy-riding." If Robert and Ackermann were still with us, we could say we had picked up

two hitchhikers. Being caught with a woman other than his wife would also account for any uneasiness Peperl might betray.

As Peperl's little car approached the designated street corner, we saw our two friends arriving from the side street, and within seconds they had got in and we were moving on.

I had given Ackermann the American money required to buy his ticket from the border to Venice and also the small amount of foreign currency that Nazi regulations would allow to be taken out of Austria. This amount would not pay for the ticket from Venice to Paris, and perhaps not even for a night's lodging in Venice. Nor was it allowed to telegraph money out of the country. I did not want to risk bringing my Dutch bank to anyone's attention; furthermore, they would not send money without my written orders and signature. However, my brother Nelson was at this time in the south of France, and I knew he would help me without asking questions. I told Ackermann that I would ask Nelson to telegraph some money to the name on Ackermann's Czech passport at the American Express office in Venice. Ackermann should then cable me an acknowledgment to Cook's Travel Office in Vienna. For some reason I did not understand, Ackermann was unwilling to use the first name given on the passport; he insisted that any telegram be addressed simply to the last name. The first name, whatever it was, seemed to embarrass him. His obstinate insistence on avoiding it was to cause complications and delay.

Although the road to Wiener Neustadt was filled with Nazi troops, we reached the station without incident, exchanged hurried farewells, and Peperl and I started back. We were not able to relax until we had turned off the main artery to continue home on country roads. Heading back toward Vienna through the open countryside, under a beautiful starry sky, we suddenly, at the same moment, looked at each other, let out a great sigh of relief, and said, with one voice, "We did it." Then we laughed. I would have liked to sing and dance. It was one of the few times I felt elated after having made it through a dangerous situation—the carnival after the morality play. Usually I had only a flat feeling of letdown when the tension had passed.

I don't think that at the time I sufficiently appreciated the courage of Peperl and Hilde Bohmer and several of our non-Jewish Austrian friends—Kaethe Gutherz, Isa Strasser, my lawyer, Dr. Kaltenegger, and others—in helping Jews and politically endangered comrades. They risked their freedom, perhaps their lives, in a completely unselfish cause. They would have to continue to live in Austria, under a Nazi regime, never for a day free from fear of arrest. It was quite different for me, who planned to leave Austria within a few months and who would, I suppose, even in the worst case, have a degree of protection by the American government. These anti-Nazi Aryans had no chance of leaving and no possibility of defying their hated government. What could they—even if thousands of them banded together—what could they do to resist, when even Schuschnigg with all his forces had not succeeded? During the following years, I heard many Americans criticize the "docile" Austrian population: "They should have protested; they should at least have left the country." How many would have loved to! How many perished in concentration camps! But, perhaps even more tragic, how many died at the front in the ranks of an army of a government they despised and loathed, fighting a war on the side they would eagerly have given heart and soul and life to fight against! These are the forgotten tragedies, the victims who seldom evoke sympathy from those at a distance. One hopes that now, after our experiences in the Indochina war, thoughtful Americans may better understand the plight of these unhappy inner-resisters of an earlier generation, who would have liked to evade, to desert, to escape, but who had no choice. Many Americans still strongly criticize those who refused to join our armed forces to fight what they considered a senseless and immoral war against Vietnam. Yet this same type of critic has no use for the anti-Nazis who did *not* desert or protest—because they could not. For them, if there was a choice at all, it was a choice of life or death. And many who had to stay risked death to help their friends.

I shall not try to relate the events of the next weeks chronologically. It must have been very soon after Ackermann left that I came home to the Rummelhardtgasse one evening at about nine to find an unfamiliar figure in the living room, comfortably seated in an easy chair, reading the newspaper. A short, dark-haired man, he rose and came toward me with a friendly manner. Holding out his hand, he introduced himself as "Leichter." Telling me he was going to Brno the next morning, he asked whether he might stay the night. I assured him that he could and asked whether he would like something to eat. Leichter replied that he had already helped himself in the kitchen. When Tony, who had let him in, joined us, I went into the kitchen to eat my supper. For the evenings when I expected to return late, Frau Kathe always left me a tray of sandwiches and a pitcher of milk, neatly covered with a clean white napkin. Having eaten nothing since noon, I lifted the cloth eagerly. The tray was there, but on it only an empty glass and plate. Obviously my equally hungry visitor had been unable to resist the tempting meal. It happened that there was not much else to eat in the apartment except crackers and a bar of chocolate.

When I returned to my guests, Leichter said he would like to go to bed since he was to catch a bus at six in the morning. I don't remember, or perhaps never knew, how he intended to get across the border. He may, like Joe, have already had a false passport. Or perhaps he planned to leave the bus on this side of the border and cross through the woods on foot at some presumably safe spot. I knew there was such a place, for Joe had crossed the border in this way at least once, guided by a Czech comrade. Whatever the plan, Leichter seemed full of confidence. I showed him to his room and asked whether he would like a sleeping pill. "Oh, no, I'm only afraid I won't wake up," he replied. "What I need is an alarm clock." I gave him one, and said good night.

Tony later described to me Leichter's arrival at the apartment. It happened that Tony's British passport was lying on the table as Leichter entered. "He was drawn to it as by a magnet," Tony told me. "He had hardly said hello when he went over to the table, picked up the passport, and studied it. I'm sure he wanted to have it, only he must have seen that the description wouldn't fit." I could not help contrasting Leichter's self-confidence and optimism, his healthy appetite and capacity for sleep, with Ackermann's timidity, anxiety, and inability to eat or sleep. I did not feel in the least critical of either comrade, but simply observed a difference in temperament in two brave men devoted to a common cause.

I had of course telegraphed Nelson the morning after Ackermann left, to ask him to send the money to Venice. I went to Cook's the following day, Thursday, hoping for a message from Ackermann, but there was none. It was not until Friday afternoon or Saturday that I received word that American Express would not deliver the money since it had been addressed to "Madame." The use of the first name of Ackermann's pseudonym would have precluded this error. Now it was necessary to telegraph Nelson once more and for him to redirect the money, which did not reach Ackermann until Monday or Tuesday. But at least we knew he was safely out of Austria.

One afternoon while visiting an elderly English friend, I met a young Englishwoman, Margaret Kaufmann, who, I found, was deeply involved in helping Jews and others in danger to leave Vienna. Our talk was almost entirely on this subject and the future of Austria and Europe. As Margaret and I took a taxi together back to the center of town, we began to talk more openly. I don't know what prompted me to mention Karl Hans Sailer, who in 1934 had been chairman of the illegal Socialist party. I was concerned about him, since I had heard—at second or third hand—that he had disappeared the night of the Anschluss. He had been on a train that had been turned back at the Czechoslovakian border, but whether Sailer had been arrested or was in hiding was not known. I had no direct connections by which to learn more. I had not expected my new acquaintance to know anything about him; it was simply a shot in the dark. But to my astonishment she told me that Sailer had managed to get off the train unobserved before it reached Vienna, that he had been in hiding and now had either left Austria or would shortly do so. Margaret had contact with Sailer's wife, Nuna, through a mutual friend, Frieda. She thought Nuna might need help, and I agreed to let Margaret give Frieda my telephone number and a password by which to identify herself.

My second trip to Brno was about a week after the first. The day and time of my arrival had been determined earlier, as had where and when I should meet Otto Bauer after settling in my hotel. But as I left the train, two familiar figures stepped forward out of the waiting crowd and greeted me warmly: Otto Bauer and Otto Leichter. I was shocked, horrified. How could they forget the simplest rules of conspiracy? Especially Leichter, who had left Nazi Austria only a few days before! Was it possible that it had not occurred to them that the Nazis might have their people watching them? Did they not realize that they were putting me in quite unnecessary danger? I told them hastily that they must let me go on alone to my hotel; that they should wait at the station as though for someone else, as though the meeting with me had been a chance one. I would meet them later at the appointed place. Leaving them as quickly as I could, I took a tram to the center of town, had coffee in a café where I could watch the people, then slipped into a rather dark church and out through a different portal and took a taxi to my hotel. As far as I could tell, no one had followed me. When I went to my rendezvous with Bauer, I was again very careful.

Bauer had five passports ready for me, two of them each for a man and wife. But there were still at least a dozen comrades, some with families, for whom passports were urgently needed. Bauer gave me good news: a Czech Socialist, Senator Heinrich Mueller, had a connection with a comrade in the Czech consulate in Vienna. This comrade would get brand-new passports for our friends. Senator Mueller would travel to Vienna to get the passports when they were ready and would then deliver them to me to distribute. It was not yet known how long it would take, but Bauer and I arranged the meeting place and passwords. I was to go to the heart clinic in the General Hospital at ten in the morning and take my place in the crowd that was always waiting there. I was to carry a paperback book: Paul de Kruif's *The Microbe Hunters.* To make contact, the senator would ask me, "Are you waiting for Dr. Schwartz?," and I was to reply, "Yes, one always has to wait a long time." I would be informed when to go to the clinic through a postcard from "Maria," mentioning the date "her vacation" would begin.

Bauer and I exchanged all our information, and on this occasion he gave me a new name, Gerda, to use in communicating with him at a safe address in Brno. I had been and still was Mary to most comrades in Vienna, Erika to Lore, Elizabeth to Bauer, and now Gerda. I had much earlier given Bauer his alias, Amos.

I took a roundabout way back to my hotel. There were few people on the street and I was confident that no one was observing me. Nevertheless, once in my room, I became suddenly very frightened when I took out the passports. Five seemed an enormous number. I tried to persuade myself that five were no more dangerous than one, even tried to joke with myself, thinking that five blueberries would be as nothing to a starving person. It was no use; I had a bad night.

I allowed myself plenty of time in the morning to tape the passports to my body and adjust my corset as carefully as possible. I was feeling a little less jittery; as always, just moving about and doing something helped.

The train stopped at the border. Instead of the usual procedure of having our passports and luggage examined in the train compartments first by Czech and then by Austrian inspectors, we were told to leave the train with all our belongings. The examination would take place in the station.

I considered for a moment the possibility of remaining on the Czech side of the border and taking a train back to Brno or some other station but discarded this idea as impractical. Since I would have to show my ticket to Vienna, the fact that I did not continue would only draw attention to me. I soon discovered that this plan would have been impossible in any case. We were guarded as we came off the train and herded immediately into a fenced-in area and from there into a line between temporary fences leading into the station. The examination on the Czech side was more or less routine, although we were carefully watched by soldiers and police. But as we passed, again between guarded fences, to the Austrian part of the station, we were told to form two lines, men in one and women and children in the other. We were to be searched.

This should have been the most frightening moment I had ever experienced. Yet, because I had to keep my head and try to save myself, I was not nearly as fearful as I had been alone in my room the night before. I did not know, as I waited in the long line, what the policewomen (Gestapo women, I corrected myself) were doing to their victims in the cubicles up ahead. If we were simply to be frisked, I thought I could chance it. But if they wanted me to strip, I would indignantly refuse and if necessary make a hell of a scene. I would scream aloud that as a citizen of the United States I would never submit to such an indignity. I was sure the crowd would sympathize with me. The German-speaking women standing in line were all grumbling, in good Austrian fashion.

As I neared the head of the line, I saw that a guard was signaling to some of the women to go ahead while diverting others to the cubicles at the side. What did this division mean? It seemed not to be based on nationality, since we had not yet shown our passports. Were those who went ahead being reprieved for some reason, or were they to be searched in other compartments further along? I asked the woman standing behind me what this meant, but she knew no more than I.

I was closer to the guard now and saw him motion to two women to go ahead, then direct one to a cubicle. The line stood still for a few moments; then the routine was repeated. I was at the head of the line when it stopped again. I thought I had recognized a pattern of letting two go on for each one who was stopped. And indeed in a moment I and the woman behind me were walking ahead to a gate where passports were being examined. "We're in luck," said the woman, coming up beside me. "It's one of those stupid spot-checks; they're searching every third person." This was one of the escapes for which I felt no elation, just a tired numbness.

Back in Vienna, I distributed the passports I had procured and got word to the others who had given me their photographs that passports for them were promised soon. One passport I brought was for Hans and Steffi Kunke, a young married couple, both teachers, but they were unwilling to leave Austria without their friend Ferdinand Tschuertsch. Tschuertsch was weak, sickly, and deformed, and it had been impossible to find anyone with a passport fitting his description. The Kunkes planned to bring their friend over the border by some illegal means. Before they were able to leave, all three were arrested in the Kunkes' apartment; all three, devoted to one another and the Socialist cause, perished in a concentration camp.

It was not long before I received the card from "Maria." On the designated day I dressed as inconspicuously as possible, took a market bag such as most Austrian women carried, and, after buying a few groceries and a newspaper, proceeded to the heart clinic. There were already twenty or thirty persons waiting. When I could find a seat, I took out

The Microbe Hunters and began to read, holding the book
so that the title could easily be seen. Every few minutes I
would pause and look around.

After a while a man standing near me asked whether I
was waiting for Dr. Schwartz. He did not look at all like a
senator but rather like a farmer or perhaps a forester who
had come to town. He was short, with graying hair and a
weather-beaten face. He wore what I remember as rather
shabby country clothes, a Tyrolean hat, and a knapsack.
"Yes, one always has to wait a long time," I replied. "Let's
step outside and get a breath of air," he said, and we left the
crowded waiting room.

I had assumed that he would simply hand me a package,
which I would put into my market bag, but instead he asked
whether there was some safe place we could go to. I told
him of the Lammgasse apartment, only five minutes away.
He questioned me closely as to its safety, seemed satisfied
with my answers, and we went up together, as usual without being seen by anyone in the building.

After we had talked for a few minutes, Senator Mueller
opened his knapsack and took out a package wrapped in
brown paper. Untying the string, he spread out twelve new
Czech passports, "legally" issued at the Czechoslovakian
consulate in Vienna. I was suddenly moved, as by some
great work of art. I felt I had never seen anything so beautiful. Tears came into my eyes; I could not speak. I don't
really know why that particular moment should have been
so breathtaking—perhaps because I had not imagined what
it would be like. It was so completely unexpected that it
had the quality of shock. As I recall this moment now, more
than forty years later, an earlier experience of thrilling surprise comes to my mind: my first sight of the Hermes of
Praxiteles at Olympia in 1925. Though I had known the
statue from photographs and from casts, I was in no way
prepared for the reality of it. The Hermes and these twelve
passports awakened in me the same dazzling rapture. Senator Mueller must have shared my emotions, because there

was an immediate feeling of harmony between us. We talked intimately for an hour or more, although we had never seen each other before, nor were we ever to meet again.

I was able to distribute these passports safely, either directly or through intermediaries. But Otto and Rosa Bauer had a new problem: for some reason—perhaps because of more stringent regulations—it would be impossible for Poldi and Rosi, their two older daughters, to cross the border on a day's pass as they had planned. Otto told me he would under no circumstances leave without his entire family. What was to be done?

We discussed all possible and impossible projects. I had the idea that I might adopt Poldi and Rosi, thus giving them American citizenship. The Bauers were acquainted with several members of the American Friends Service Committee (which had first begun to help Austria in 1919, immediately after World War I). I also knew the committee, including Emma Cadbury, a most sympathetic and helpful person, and thought they might be able to advise me how to go about adopting the girls. However, these kind and wise Quakers convinced me that it would be impossible, and I later wondered how I had ever thought there was a chance. But there are situations in which one is bound to try to make the impossible possible.

When I saw Otto again, he had another proposal: a Czech friend of his, a professor in Prague, had two daughters about the ages of Poldi and Rosi. Otto thought they might have passports that his girls could use. (I am puzzled now why there was no problem about exchanging photographs—but I know we did not consider it a difficulty. Possibly as minors on a Czech family passport they did not require photographs.) I agreed to travel to Prague that weekend.

I got a berth on a night train on Saturday, which brought me to Prague very early the next morning. I breakfasted in a comfortable hotel, then read the newspapers until a respectable hour for a Sunday-morning call, when I made my way on foot to the professor's home.

He received me kindly, as one of Otto's friends, but he seemed bewildered. Although he, like Otto, belonged to the League of Religious Socialists, I think he was out of touch with the whole political situation. I explained everything carefully, emphasizing the danger Otto was in and how important it was for him to get away. The professor listened attentively, sadly shaking his head. When I came to the problem of passports for Poldi and Rosi, I had the feeling that he did not grasp its urgency. The professor and his family had no valid passports, and it turned out that our scheme was impossible anyhow—I can't quite remember why. Concerned about the professor's future, I asked him whether he had any fears that Czechoslovakia would be the next victim of Hitler's power drive. He said he had never thought about it. Before leaving, I urged him to get passports for himself and his family in case of danger. I felt some hesitation in speaking in this way about his country and its future, but this was no moment to care whether he found me officious.

Discouraged, I walked away sadly, thinking of the Bauers and trying to find some solution to their problem, but nothing occurred to me. After walking half an hour or so, I began to wonder what I should do with myself the rest of the day. I had been in Prague before and really loved this wonderful city, but I was in no mood to appreciate its beauties. Nor did I feel like wandering about the streets, as I would have done at another time. It was a cold, damp, dark Sunday, and my spirits matched the day. I would have to pass the time somehow until my train left in the evening. I had never acquired the habit of dropping into a movie when I had time on my hands. I would have to sit over lunch and dinner with a book, for as long as possible, and in the afternoon sit in a café. (Years later, in the same mood on an equally sad and dreary Sunday in Moscow, when I had exhausted my reading matter and there was no warm, hospitable café where I could sit, I looked back on that day in Prague almost with nostalgia.)

When at last the evening came I boarded the Vienna train

as soon as it was made up and was asleep in my berth when we came to the border. The Czech passport official who came into my compartment made only a cursory examination. The Austrian who followed studied my passport closely and looked at me suspiciously. "What were you doing in Prague?" he asked. "Sightseeing," I replied. "I shall soon be returning to America, and I wanted to see Prague before I leave." "What! This long journey for only a few hours!" "No, I had a lovely long day there; I arrived early yesterday morning." "You arrived there today, Sunday," he contradicted me. How stupid of me! I had supposed that the border was much nearer to Vienna and thought my passport would be stamped as leaving Austria on Saturday and returning Monday. But I was indeed crossing in both directions on the same day, Sunday. "I mean this morning, then, if it's still Sunday," I replied. "I left Vienna Saturday evening, since I prefer traveling by sleeping-car, and it saves me the hotel bill. One long day in Prague was just right." He was still not satisfied and questioned me closely on what I had done and seen. I mentioned the principal sights of the city and the famous restaurant where I had eaten lunch. Finally he left me, still shaking his head.

I must explain that I myself had two passports, both legally issued. Since I first began to travel, I had, of course, had an American passport. When Connie (whose father was English) was born in March 1931, I had tried to get her a British passport, since at that time, according to both British and American law, a child had the nationality of the father. The British, however, refused to issue a separate passport for an infant of three months and insisted that I obtain a British passport for Connie and myself together. According to their law, I, having married an Englishman, was British. However, to the United States I was still American, and America did not at that time recognize dual citizenship. This situation made me very uneasy, since I feared I might lose my American citizenship if I admitted to having a British passport. But there was no other way of getting a passport for Connie. So, with some trepidation, I accepted, and we all traveled to the United States on British passports. A few years later I was able to get a separate passport for Connie. The British consul recalled our joint passport and as a matter of course issued a separate one for me. These passports were good for five years and could be extended for another five, I believe. I now found it very convenient to have two passports, which I could use alternately for my travels and thus avoid the appearance of crossing the border as often as I did.

Back in Vienna, there were a hundred things to do. I have no idea of the sequence of the tasks I was faced with. One day Steffi came to me. I had not known her before, but she was the fiancée of a man for whom I had obtained one of the first passports. He had gone to Paris, and Steffi was determined to join him. I could no longer get passports through our comrades in Czechoslovakia and did not know what to suggest. As Steffi and I sat talking, it occurred to me that the description on my passport—brown eyes, brown hair—could apply to her. It is true she was not so tall as I, but height in feet and inches meant little to passport examiners familiar only with the metric system. There was of course no possibility of exchanging photographs, but I thought that Steffi, with a hat and scarf and a little luck, could pass for the person in the photograph. I brought out my English passport, and we discussed it. To my surprise, this plucky woman did not hesitate. She asked just two questions: "How shall I get it back to you?" and "What shall I say if I am caught?" I told her that, as I would soon be traveling to Paris on my other passport, I would pick up the one she used there. We agreed that in case she was apprehended for traveling on a passport not her own, she would say she had stolen it, and we worked out the details. Fortunately, this precaution was not necessary. Everything proceeded without a hitch, and I retrieved the precious document on my next journey to Paris. Both passports were by this time so marked up with stamps of departures and entrances that it would have been impossible, without the most careful scrutiny, to ascertain that there had not been a return journey.

In the months following the Anschluss I traveled to Paris and Switzerland several times. I always had many messages to exchange between comrades in Austria and Paris. But the principal purpose of my first journey to Paris was to take K and Silva Lake's son, Pups, to join Connie in Arosa. There was much to talk over with Joe and the other comrades, but I could not stay away from Vienna for long. After two or three days in Paris, some of the time spent with the Lakes, I took Pups on the night train to Sargans, where Connie and Fini were waiting for him at the station. I had time only to step out and embrace Connie, promise to visit them soon, and say good-bye before continuing on the same train to Vienna.

Some time after this Frieda, the Sailers' friend to whom Margaret Kaufmann had given my name, called me and we arranged an hour for her to come to the Rummelhardtgasse. She arrived, accompanied—somewhat to my dismay—by Nuna Sailer. Bringing Nuna to me seemed a quite unnecessary risk. I was trying to minimize the number of people known to have been involved in illegal activity who came to my apartment. There were already too many, but in most cases it had been unavoidable.

Nuna's case was complicated, not only because it was known that her husband had fled, but also because she had a child about six months old. Frieda was trying to persuade her to get away at once if at all possible and leave the child with Frieda until a way could be found to send him after her. This seemed to me sensible; Nuna would almost certainly be in danger if she remained much longer. Once again the thought struck me that my extra passport could be of use; her description matched mine—brown hair, brown eyes, about the same age. Perhaps there was even a slight resemblance between us. I produced the passport, which I had brought back a week or so earlier, and asked Nuna whether she wanted to use it. At first she and Frieda rejected the idea completely. I was unwilling to urge her but had to say that I knew of no other way to get her a passport. I told her that it had already been used successfully by a person who resembled me less than she did. I knew that a few people without passports had crossed the mountains into Switzerland on skis. To attempt to do so, however, one had to be a first-rate skier and also know the safest places to cross. I could try to get more information for her. But both Nuna and Frieda discarded this idea as impossible.

They studied my passport again and asked me a good many questions. I suggested that, if Nuna decided to use it, she should take a berth in a *wagon-lit*, which would cross the border at night. The examination was usually more superficial for sleeping-car passengers; furthermore, the lights in the sleeping compartments were bad. I could give her a suitcase with my initials, M.M.G., if that would make her feel safer. I also thought she should carry a pair of skis and buy her rail ticket to some Swiss ski resort. After much discussion, Nuna decided to risk it. But I would not let them take the passport and suitcase with them that evening. They had come directly from Nuna's apartment and could not be sure that they hadn't been followed. I charged Frieda to come alone the next day from her home, without having been at Nuna's, and to watch carefully.

Frieda came the next afternoon and told me that all had been arranged. She had been at the station and bought Nuna a ticket to Davos. Frieda was going to keep Nuna's baby, and they had worked out all the necessary details. And, indeed, everything succeeded according to plan. Frieda came to me some days later—this time unannounced—to tell me that Nuna was safe in Paris. Although I was irritated by Frieda's lack of caution, I could not help admiring her warmhearted devotion to her friend. And it turned out that Frieda did me and the Bauers a great service in a quite unexpected way.

I cannot remember what Frieda or I said that led to our discussing the problem of the two Bauer girls. I had been thinking that if the right official at the Czech consulate could be approached, he might add Poldi's and Rosi's names to the family passport, but I had no idea who such a person might be or how he might be contacted. Amazingly, I found that Frieda knew the right person to talk to! What I cannot understand now is why she had not approached him for a passport for Nuna. There are many such gaps in my memory, where I still know the facts but not the reasons. Possibly Frieda learned only then that false passports were issued and felt sure that it must have been done by the comrade she knew. In any case, after I had given to Frieda the passport and photographs from the Bauers, she brought a passport back, properly made out for the whole family.

By now it was early April, and it was becoming more difficult daily to leave the country. Anyone of any nationality who had been in Austria for even a few days was now required to have a receipt from the Austrian revenue service indicating that he had paid his taxes or that no taxes were due from him and present it at the border. I had obtained such a statement for myself but had not yet had to show it, although I had crossed at least once since this regulation had been in effect. But it was quite impossible for the Bauers to get any such receipt, and what if they should be asked for it? They would have to take their chances; if it was demanded, they would have to try to bluff or bribe the officials. I decided that I would travel by the same train, in a neighboring compartment. There was a slim chance that I could be of help. If the officials asked for my tax receipt I could say that I had never heard of this order, that it was not well publicized, that it was unfair, that this red tape was ruining Austria's tourist trade; I might be treated leniently since in those days an American passport often evoked respect. And if they let me proceed (possibly paying a fine), the occupants of the next carriage could bolster their arguments with mine.

It seemed best to take tickets to Venice, from which we could proceed to Zurich. We left Vienna in the evening. At the station I waited outside the train until I saw the six Bauers settled in a third-class carriage; then I took a place in the compartment next to theirs. The trip to the border, although probably not more than about six hours, seemed endless. The Austrian examination, for my friends as well as for me, was routine; tax receipts were never mentioned. Next came the Italian officials, and for a moment I experienced an irrational wave of fear—they looked so sinister in their Fascist uniforms. Then they too were gone and the train began to move. I stepped into the corridor and smiled at the Bauers through the glass door. But Otto, by an almost imperceptible shake of the head, cautioned me to show no recognition; we were in a Fascist country; perhaps my fears had not been altogether irrational. I went back to my compartment to try to sleep.

We reached Venice in the morning, separately checked our bags at the station, and boarded the first *vaporetto* to the Piazza San Marco. Only after we were there did we greet each other and sit down together for refreshment. We had decided to take the overnight train to Zurich, and I bought our tickets at the American Express. Then I cabled Joe, who was going to meet me there, and Otto cabled his Swiss friends. I had never supposed that any day spent in Venice could seem long, but this one dragged on interminably. We were all tired and spent; we hardly had the energy to talk. It was good to board the train in the evening and still better to arrive at the Zurich station early the next morning. Otto's friends gasped in joyful surprise as they saw all six Bauers descend from the train. His cable had been signed only "Otto," and they had thought he was coming alone.

Friedrich and Kathia Adler were in Zurich, and through them we met a Swiss couple, Mr. and Mrs. F., who were eager to help their Austrian comrades. I thought of the Sailer baby. Mrs. F. assured me that she would be able to find a Swiss comrade with a baby who could get a passport for herself and her child. She could then travel alone to Vienna and return to Zurich, bringing the Sailer baby with her.

Thankfully I gave Mrs. F. my address, and we arranged that the comrade would come to me and that I would contact Frieda. "Look at this bag," said Mrs. F., handing me a rather unusual leather handbag that she was wearing on a shoulder strap. "Whoever comes to you for the baby will be wearing this bag." Early one morning a few weeks later I opened the door of my Vienna apartment to a pleasant young woman wearing this bag, who took the Sailer baby safely to Zurich.

Otto Leichter was also in Zurich. He implored me to do everything possible to persuade his wife, Kaethe, to leave Austria at once. Their two young sons were fortunately out of the country. But Kaethe, although she had one of the new Czech passports, was delaying her departure. She had apparently been told by the Gestapo that if she tried to leave the country her mother would be interned. All her friends knew that Kaethe would certainly be arrested if she stayed, and perhaps her mother would be also. Kaethe herself, a highly intelligent Jewish woman who had been a prominent political figure in her own right, surely knew this too. Still, it must have been a difficult decision to make. Every hour she remained increased the danger. It was said also that Kaethe delayed in the hope of saving some of their possessions. Although some people did this, feeling that their whole future depended upon their having the means of making a new start in some other country, one would not expect it of Kaethe.

Otto was rightly in despair. He asked me to get in touch with a certain Maria Weigl in Vienna and give her messages to take to Kaethe from "Onkel Stefan." It happened that I knew Maria fairly well; she, like Gerda and Fini, was a young kindergarten teacher trained in the Anna Freud tradition and was now governess to the Bibring children. I had not known that Maria had any connection with the Leichters or with any illegal work. And she, when we met on my return to Vienna, was even more amazed by my bringing a message from a comrade known to her as "Onkel Stefan." She did her utmost, as did other friends, to persuade Kaethe

Leichter to leave Austria—but to no avail. Kaethe was arrested and perished in a Nazi concentration camp. This unnecessary tragedy was one of the saddest of all. The day after Kaethe's arrest, her mother committed suicide.

After a few busy days in Zurich, I went to Arosa to be with Connie and Pups. Although I was there for only a short time, these days were both a pleasure in themselves and a much-needed vacation from care and anxiety. I could really relax and enjoy the children, the mountains, and Arosa's splendid sunshine. The snow was still deep on the ski slopes, but spring had come to the valleys below the village. One day we took a picnic lunch and walked down the mountain into masses of flowers. Wild crocuses covered the meadows up to the very edge of the snow.

What a satisfaction it was to see that both children were happy! Pups was almost three years older than Connie, but he was young for ten and Connie was in some ways mature for seven. Both were blessed with a tremendous curiosity, a desire for knowledge in every imaginable field. Both also had a considerable love of mischief—not such a blessing for Fini, who, with her gentle manner, often had difficulty coping with their pranks. This early acquaintance with Pups (whom I had hardly seen since his infancy) was the prelude to a friendship that has deepened through the years. I am touched by his devotion—springing from this visit, which he remembers as the happiest experience of his childhood— to us all.

Hard as it was to leave Arosa, I was not sorry to be back in Vienna. There was so much to be done! Now that many of our political friends had left, I would have more time for other friends, as well as for some personal matters. For instance, I had to get rid of the many volumes of Marx and Lenin in my little, locked cupboard in the Lammgasse. With a heavy heart I packed the books into a cheap suitcase, which I took in a taxi to a railroad station and deposited in the parcel room. I then destroyed the check and dropped the key into the canal. There was still some clothing of Joe's stuffed

into the same cupboard. When Tony Hyndman had left Vienna some time earlier, he had taken a few of the clothes
with him and delivered or mailed them to Joe. But now I
had to get rid of the rest, including Joe's best and favorite
suit, a nice gray herringbone tweed that I had helped him
buy in London. I knew that Joe's brother Tony, who lived
in Stockerau not far from Vienna, could wear Joe's clothes
and decided to try to get them to him. So again I packed a
suitcase and deposited it in the Franz Josef Station, the terminal of the Stockerau trains. This time I mailed the key
and check to Tony, hoping that he would figure out that he
was to collect the deposited object. We had no way of knowing, until we saw Tony after the war, that he had done so.
Although Joe approved of my strategy, he could not quite
conceal his disappointment that I had not somehow managed to salvage his favorite suit. No other suit ever equaled
it in his esteem.

It was on one of these April days that I met "the Wolf-
Man" by chance on the street. He had been a wealthy young
Russian who had come to Vienna in 1910 to be analyzed by
Freud and was the subject of Freud's famous *History of an
Infantile Neurosis*. After the Russian Revolution he returned to Vienna and was later in analysis with Ruth Mack
Brunswick. To preserve his anonymity, Freud and others
who have written about the case referred to him as "the
Wolf-Man," since wolves played a large part in his dreams,
fantasies, and fears. I had taken weekly lessons in Russian
from him for a year or two in the late 1920s, but in recent
years I had seen him only occasionally, in connection with
my insurance policies, since he worked in the company that
issued them. Now, greeting me on the street, he began to
cry loudly. I invited him up to my nearby apartment and
finally learned his story through his sobs: his wife had committed suicide.

I did not know what to do to help the Wolf-Man in his
distress except listen to him. At first I thought his wife's
suicide might be politically motivated; there were many

suicides in Vienna in those early Nazi days. But this was apparently not the case. In fact the Wolf-Man seemed remarkably unconcerned about the Nazi takeover; he was, indeed, unconcerned about everything except his wife's death and his own state of despair.

My first thought was, naturally, that he needed an analyst, but Dr. Brunswick had left Austria and most other analysts had left or were preparing to leave as soon as possible. I knew of no one he could turn to. Then, remembering that Dr. Brunswick would be in Paris and London during the summer, I suggested to the Wolf-Man that he try to see her in those two cities. He was eager to do so, and now began another and quite arduous task for me: to help him make all the arrangements.

The first thing to do was to write or cable Dr. Brunswick, to make sure she could see the Wolf-Man. She replied affirmatively, giving the dates she would be in both Paris and London. It was necessary for the Wolf-Man, who was a man without a country, without nationality, to procure some sort of travel document. He was finally given a document for stateless people, called a Nansen passport, and could now apply for visas for England and France. He needed only a visitor's visa, since he would of course return to Austria, but both France and England were wary about granting any visas at all. Furthermore, it was extremely difficult even to get into their consulates. Queues lined the streets day and night. I had written to various friends in England and France, including Princess Marie Bonaparte, Freud's pupil and friend, whom I had met a few times, for letters of invitation and the necessary guarantees. Everything took time, and the Wolf-Man's problems were still far from settled when I left Austria in late June, although he may have had his French visa by this time. I had spent more than one long day with him waiting in line on the street. I remember that when we finally got into the British consulate the young woman receiving us—British-born as far as I could judge—made several very anti-Semitic remarks. Since the Wolf-Man was not

Jewish they did not affect him directly, but the incident shocked and angered me so that I had a hard time curbing my inclination to answer sharply. Knowing that this could only damage his chances, I forced myself to hold my tongue. He finally did get to Paris in August, and later to London, where his daily hour with Dr. Brunswick helped him to survive the tragedy that had affected him so deeply.

Of my personal friends still in Austria, I was most concerned about the Urbachs. They had no immediate prospects of leaving; either they could not get an exit permit or thought it too dangerous to try. We met frequently and discussed all kinds of schemes; none seemed feasible. When I left Vienna in late June, I had to leave them behind. The Urbachs had several devoted Aryan friends who would, I knew, do anything within their power to help them. One was Isa Strasser, to whom I had introduced them. Another was Kaethe Gutherz, an old friend of theirs who had acted as Connie's governess one summer when Fini took a long vacation. Before I left Vienna, Kaethe and I made plans to meet in Zurich sometime in the future if for any reason a meeting would help to facilitate the Urbachs' leaving. We were to meet on the steps of the central post office at twelve noon on a date that would be mentioned in some other connection on a postcard. If one of us did not turn up at noon, the other was to reappear there at two o'clock, then at four, then at six. This meeting did indeed take place according to plan, but not until March 1939, when I had been in Paris for more than eight months. I had procured a British passport for Annie Urbach from one of Stephen Spender's friends, and one for Franz and their little son, Johnnie, from a Welsh friend who had a son about Johnnie's age. There was of course no possibility of changing the photographs, but the descriptions matched extraordinarily well.

Kaethe stayed for a few days with us in Switzerland, then returned with the passports to Vienna, but she had already told me she did not think the Urbachs would use them. I, too, was doubtful; Annie might be willing, but probably not

Franz. It would be a serious risk because of his "top secret" work, but remaining in Vienna might be even more dangerous. Kaethe was right; the passports were never used; they were, I suppose, destroyed. A few months later, the Urbachs found a safer and better way to leave. With the help of a colleague of Franz's, a friendly Nazi party member, and my Aryan lawyer, with whom I had left some American money for such purposes, they were able to proceed to Sweden. In December 1939, they came to the United States.

People whom I knew only slightly or not at all also came to me for help or advice. One was a bright, attractive young Jewish woman, Hilda F., whom I had never seen before. She was the youngest in a family consisting of a mother and four daughters. One way still open to women wanting to leave Austria was to get a contract with an English person or family for work as a domestic servant. Through Stephen and his generous, sympathetic friends, I was able to get such contracts for a number of women, including, I believe, all five F.s. Hilda and a sister, Franzi, went on to the United States, and I saw them there when I went to New York for three months in the spring of 1939. It was, however, a terribly sad meeting. Franzi had indicated on the telephone that something was the matter, that Hilda was very changed. When I saw her she was apathetic and withdrawn and would hardly speak. I realized this must be schizophrenia. It was my first experience of seeing this change in a person whom I had known as a healthy, animated human being, and it was hard for me to get over the shock. I took Hilda to a psychiatrist, and she was hospitalized and, I believe, given insulin shock treatments. Letters from Franzi after I returned to Paris told me her sister was improving. Then came a letter saying that Hilda, still in the hospital, had died. The diagnosis was tuberculosis.

Writing now about my last months in Vienna, from April to June 1938, many, many memories come back to me, often of people I knew only in that "crowded hour." Many of them I have not thought about in years; there are even some whose names I have forgotten. But some have kept in touch with me ever since.

One, who has become a friend, though I seldom see her, was a medical student in my class. Stefanie, as I shall call her, was a slight, pretty girl with light gold-red hair, a person of obvious intelligence and great charm. We had met on the way to Dr. Erdheim's pathology class, which took place every Saturday morning at the Lainz Hospital. It was a popular class, and one had to be there soon after six A.M. to get a good seat and then wait and wait. Since Lainz was almost an hour's ride by streetcar from where we both lived, we had to start out frightfully early. My first meeting with Stefanie occurred when we got off the same tram and walked together the five or ten minutes to the classroom. Riding back together in the tram, we became better acquainted. I told Stefanie that I had a little daughter and that it was hard to combine family life with my medical studies and do justice to both. I am sure that it was in response to this that Stefanie made me a very kind offer: she would always go early to the Lainz Hospital and save me a place so I could arrive just in time for the lecture. This favor did indeed make my Saturdays much easier.

I had not seen Stefanie for many months, since our pathology classes were behind us, when I met her by chance on the street one day in late May or early June 1938. I was happy to see her, but she looked troubled. I invited her to come up to my apartment to talk. It had never occurred to me to consider whether Stefanie (or anyone I met) was Jewish since I had grown up in an atmosphere completely devoid of anti-Semitism and had attended a girls' school in Chicago composed about equally of Jews and Gentiles. Now Stefanie told me that she was Jewish, was doubtful whether she would be allowed to take her final medical examinations and graduate in Vienna, and was trying to get a visa to the United States. If I remember correctly, she had hopes of getting an affidavit from a distant relative in the United States but was unwilling to leave without her fiancé, Karl.

Stefanie had written the American cousin a long letter about this, which she had with her. She had been worrying about whether she had said the right things in the letter, and also about whom she could get to translate it into English, when our chance meeting occurred. I was very moved by the letter, which I translated for her. I told Stefanie I would have been happy to give Karl an affidavit, but the American consul in Vienna would not accept any more from me, claiming I had already given too many. I had written to all the members of my family asking for affidavits for our politically endangered friends. Although many of these friends were now in Switzerland or France, they could not remain in those countries permanently and we were trying to get them to the United States. I promised Stefanie that when I arrived in Paris I would try to find a way for Karl to get out of Austria to one country or another, but warned her that this was becoming more and more difficult. It was almost impossible to get into either France or Switzerland unless one had a visa, or the promise of a visa, to proceed to some other country.

Stefanie and Karl were unexpectedly allowed to take their examinations later that summer and were married in the fall. Stefanie, who had received her affidavit, went to Switzerland. At some point I found a consul somewhere who would accept an affidavit from me for Karl. Both were still waiting for their quota numbers to come up when war broke out. When Stefanie's quota number came up she was told she had to return to Vienna within three days to get her visa; otherwise she would lose her quota number. Returning entailed a tremendous risk, since there was a big *J* for Jew stamped in her passport, and more especially since at that very time Germany (which by then included Austria, of course) had temporarily closed all its borders. At the German border, Stefanie refused to turn back. At last her courage impressed the authorities, and they made an exception to allow her to continue, the only woman in a train full of German troops. She got her visa, saw Karl briefly, and returned at once to Switzerland. There were more difficulties at the border, but someone again took pity on her and directed her to walk a mile or so along a certain lonely road; she would then be on Swiss soil. Courage and luck had saved the visa.

Stefanie and Karl, who got his visa soon afterward, met in Italy and sailed from there to the United States, arriving just before Christmas in 1939. They have been practicing medicine here ever since.

Whenever I think back about this one example of so many senseless troubles—and most of them I have omitted—I get angry at the absolutely unnecessary bureaucratic meannesses that cause so much individual misery. There seems no reason at all why the American consul in Zurich could not have issued the visa to Stefanie there.

One day an unfamiliar woman came to my apartment. She introduced herself as Frau Kalischer, the wife of Cornelius, who had been arrested. There was some hope of getting him out of Austria if he could get a visa to another country. This appeal, too, came at a time when my affidavits were no longer accepted. His was a desperate situation, and I cannot now forgive myself for not having made greater efforts to get an affidavit for him. I should have asked Nelson, who had always been so bountiful in his gifts and who later told me spontaneously: "I'll give you a whole bunch of affidavits." But I was at that time hesitant to ask anyone for more than one affidavit. Hardly any of my friends were in a position to guarantee even one person, although when I later appealed to them many generously responded, either by giving an affidavit themselves or by obtaining one or more through their friends. Cornelius was a special case: I was reluctant to ask any friend to guarantee his support for five years because I knew his character defects, his unreliability in regard to money. Sorrowfully I told Frau Kalischer that I could not get an affidavit for Cornelius. She thought it might be possible to get a visa to Australia if she could pay the passage. I promised the money for the passage if she

could obtain the visa and thus eased my conscience a little.
But this attempt was unsuccessful, and Cornelius perished
in a concentration camp.

It was my scruples about asking anyone to guarantee that
Cornelius would never become "a public charge" that prevented me from doing my best to save him. Are these scruples valid, face-to-face with death? I think now that I was
wrong. I could have promised the person from whom I asked
the affidavit that I would foot the bill. And in fact I made
such promises several times later to persons who could give
an affidavit only under these conditions. Somehow I should
have found a way. Certainly I should have tried harder. This
is the one instance for which I feel guilt. But, even more
than guilt, an immeasurable sadness.

Many Jewish friends asked me to take jewelry out of the
country for them, and this I was always able to do, with no
uneasiness, carrying it in a little jewel case with my initials.
It was never examined. However, when a dentist whose excellent cram course I had attended begged me to take out
his supply of gold, I had to refuse; it would have been risking
too much. Dr. Adler, my gynecologist and teacher, had a
different errand for me: to get word to his bank in Holland
not to send him any money or communications. He dared
not mail such a letter from Vienna, nor would it have been
wise for me to carry it. We finally devised a plan. Dr. Adler
wrote me a reference for my medical work, leaving a blank
space of several lines before his signature. In Paris I cut off
the reference and in the space above his name typed in the
directions to the bank and mailed it. It was a very little
thing, but for him it meant future security in America.

The university opened in early May and I signed up for
my next two examinations, a week apart. There would still
be two more to take, for which I was not yet well prepared.
I had not opened a book since March 11. Of the four professors whom I had expected to examine me, two—both
Jewish—had been replaced. One of them had committed suicide; the other had "disappeared." Whether he had been ar-

rested or had fled the country I never learned. I passed the first two examinations and began cramming for the others. Alex Rogawski, an Austrian student whom I knew slightly as a good friend of Harold Harvey's, offered to tutor and test me, much as Harold and I had done for each other. Alex, however, had already finished his studies, so he was doing me a purely one-sided favor. His tutoring was a tremendous help to me, not only in learning the material for my ophthalmology and dermatology exams, but also as a stimulus to complete a certain stint every day.

I got to know Alex better and liked him very much. He had an affidavit for the United States from Harold's sister Minnie and was hoping to get to Sweden to await his quota turn there. I was enormously grateful for his help and would have liked to pay him, but I dared not even suggest this. He had offered his help as an act of friendship, and I was afraid of offending him. This was not the only case where a false embarrassment on my part prevented me from offering a deserved and much needed remuneration. I think now that it was a mistake in my upbringing that allowed me to feel there could be anything degrading or embarrassing in such an exchange. A few such experiences I was never able to rectify, but fortunately in Alex's case I was able months later to show him an act of friendship: when he was in Sweden I sent him a hundred dollars. He told me later that he had been literally destitute when this unexpected gift arrived. In New York, in 1940 or 1941, Alex and I met by chance on the street. He was living in a small, dark room not far from Joe and me, and we were happy to let him study for his New York medical boards in our apartment.

After passing my last examination, I was faced with the really hard job of getting together the many documents required to allow me to graduate from the Vienna Medical School. Getting through Austrian bureaucracy had always been an ordeal; now that the red tape was compounded with Nazi demands, it had become a nightmare. I cannot remember all the things that had to be done or in what order, but

I know that I stood in line at the various university offices for many hours, spread over several days.

Jews were not being allowed to graduate with the Aryans in mid-June, although there were vague rumors that at least the American Jews might be given a separate graduation later. No one knew what would happen. Although my father was of Jewish descent, I had been brought up a Protestant and had never thought of myself as Jewish. When registering with the Austrian police, as one had to do whenever changing one's residence even for a single night, I had for years written "Protestant" under the heading "religion," and later— when I learned that there was such a thing—I wrote *"Konfessionslos,"* meaning "without affiliation." At the university I was given a long form to fill out about my ancestry, baptism, marriage, everything imaginable. The easiest thing, and the only sensible thing, would have been simply to write that my parents and grandparents were all Protestants. Certainly I had no scruples about lying to the Nazis, and in this case there was not the slightest danger that a lie would be detected. But I felt a sudden, unexpected sense of solidarity with my American colleagues, all of whom were Jewish. I don't know why I felt this. I barely knew them, had no personal ties with any of them, and did not consider myself a Jew. But I wrote "Jewish" as my father's religion. I think now that this was a senseless thing to do; it could only hurt me and also make me less useful to my friends. It did no one any good. I ask myself now what impelled me to this irrational, injudicious act. I cannot believe that it was a sudden upsurge of Jewish identity, which I had never felt before and have never felt since. Was it a passionate need to identify with the oppressed? I have no answer.

I knew at the time, of course, that this deed might preclude my graduation. Even if American Jews were given a later date, it might not be advisable for me to remain longer in Vienna. In the last months I had had so many encounters, without proper precautions, with people who might well be suspect that I was eager to leave as soon as possible. After

handing in this form I was kept waiting for several days
until called for an interview by the dean or some other official. He questioned me in great detail and finally told me
that, although I was a *"Mischling ersten Grades"*—a "person of mixed race, first degree"—it had been decided to allow me to graduate since it was not my mother but my
father who was a Jew and since my former husband had been
a Protestant. However, I was forced to sign a paper stating
that I would never practice medicine in Austria even if I
acquired citizenship.

The final standing in line at another window should have
been quite easy; it was simply a matter of producing proof
of the date and place of my birth and my nationality. However, the examiner at this window was a minor university
employee, a sort of porter, who happened to be both ignorant
and stubborn. The line moved slowly, as the porter spent
excessive time studying each form and accompanying document. When my turn came I handed him the form I had
filled out, with my American passport as proof. He studied
both carefully. "You were born in Chicago?" "Yes," I replied. "Your nationality?" "American." "South American?"
"No, North American. United States of America." "You must
be South American," the porter remonstrated. "Chicago is
in South America." "No, it is in Illinois, in North America."
We argued for a few minutes. When I pointed out that my
passport was from the United States, he must have thought
I was trying to deceive him and told me rudely to go along.
By this time the students behind me were impatiently hoot-
ing and shouting for me to move on. But I was not about to
give up in this ridiculous skirmish. I asked the porter for an
atlas, to show him where Chicago was, and was relieved
that he was able to produce one. But he kept the atlas on
his side of the window, looking near-sightedly at the map
of South America. More minutes passed. I thought the crowd
would mob me, and I didn't blame them. Sticking my hand
through the little arch in the window, I seized the atlas and
opened it to the United States, pointing out Chicago to the

porter. Reluctantly, he gave me the final necessary stamps and seals, and I bolted out of the building.

Graduation took place on the eighteenth of June. It was of course not the ceremony that I cared about but getting the diploma. The ceremony, in fact, I found quite distressing, since we were graduating from a Nazi university and were expected to raise our arms and say "Heil Hitler." The only foreign student other than myself was from India. This student, whom I knew from classes and who was never sure of the answer to even the simplest question, now asked me whether or not he should say "Heil Hitler." I replied that I could not tell him what to do. Was I going to? No. What did I think he ought to do? I never did find out what he did since he stood in a row behind me. However, we both got our diplomas.

I was now ready to leave, except for packing. I had been given permission to take my personal belongings and furniture out of the country on the condition that two Nazi officials supervise the packing of trunks and boxes in my apartment and their loading into approved vans. I had to pay these two men by the hour, as they hovered unpleasantly over me and the packers. At length all was completed. Frau Lucy, Augenfeld's former maid, took Connie's canary for her young daughter; she also kept Klecks, our little dachshund, until we were settled in Paris. I said good-bye to my friends.

Five days after my arrival in Paris Joe received a letter from Lore and I one from Dr. Kaltenegger, my lawyer. Both warned me under no circumstances to return to Vienna. The Gestapo was searching for me. Kaltenegger added that they believed me to be a foreign agent.

Four

Going Home:
Paris, from June 1938
to November 1939

On my way to Paris I stopped for a day or two in Switzerland to see Connie and Pups. They had moved to a hotel on the shore of the beautiful Lake Lucerne after the mountain snows had melted. The children and Fini joined Joe and me in Paris a week or so later, when I had found living quarters for us all.

In Switzerland i had to get myself a French visa. (Either this was a new requirement for Americans or else my old visa had expired.) As I expected to make Paris my residence for some time, I wanted to enter on my American passport and register there as an American. But it had been impossible to get into the French consulate in Vienna; I would probably have had to stand in line for twenty-four hours or more on the street. I found out that there was a French consulate in Zug, not far from Lucerne, and stopped off for a few hours there. However, the consul at this small office was unable to give me a regular visa. He offered me a transit visa, assuring me that in France I would have no difficulty getting it changed to a regular one. Unfortunately I accepted this assertion; it was to cause me no end of bother in the coming year.

In Paris I found Joe extremely busy with the complicated politics of the Foreign Board of the Austrian Socialists, of which he was chairman. Besides the comrades who had left Austria after the Anschluss, almost all of the "old" group, in exile in Brno since 1934, had by now come to Paris. There were differences of opinion and open dissension not only between the old and the new emigrants but also among the members of the "new" party. Joe was worried and often gloomy, not the cheerful, active, even-tempered person I had known in Austria.

During the next fifteen months I became more and more dissatisfied. I felt that Joe was wasting his time and talents on fruitless arguments; I would have liked him to resign from the Foreign Board long before he did. This preference was not altogether a rational political criticism on my part, since I recognized Joe's reasons for remaining; it was, rather, a matter of temperament. The concessions and compromises he had to make as chairman, even if wise and expedient, were repugnant to me, and I felt Joe could be using his time and ability for something more worthwhile. He must often have felt this way himself but considered it his duty to remain, not only as a loyal Socialist but also to hold the party together. But it was not a happy period for either of us.

Lore's letter warning me not to return to Vienna brought more bad news: Holoubek, who had promised to leave Austria that very week, had been arrested. Besides the anguish we felt for Holoubek personally, Joe experienced his absence as a great loss in his work in Paris; of all the comrades still in Austria, Holoubek was closest to Joe in his political ideas.

Within a few days another blow struck us—the sudden death of Otto Bauer. Both Joe and I had had a personal attachment to as well as admiration for this great man.

Very soon after my arrival in Paris, I learned that Joe assumed we were going to marry. This came as rather a shock to me and even frightened me a little. It having been quite impossible for us to marry during our years together in Austria, I don't believe I had ever considered it. I do remember that a few years earlier an American friend, meeting Joe for the first time and seeing the love in his eyes and in mine, asked me whether I thought I would marry him. I replied: "No, but I think we'll live together happily ever after." I am sure it suited me that the question of marriage never arose. I had really never wanted to marry, except for the purpose of having children and providing them with two legitimate parents and a home. Otherwise, I preferred a love relationship without bonds.

Now, although I believed that Joe was the only man with whom I would want to spend my entire life, I nevertheless felt some reluctance. Expediency dictated my decision, however: marriage to an American would greatly facilitate Joe's entry into the United States and obtaining American citizenship. It would give him some sort of nationality status. He had renounced his former citizenship (since the Anschluss Austrians were automatically German) upon arrival in Paris, and in any case he possessed no legal papers. We set about preparing to marry.

This was more difficult than we had supposed. Neither of us had a *carte d'identité*. We both spent hours at the prefecture and at various ministries, to no avail. Because I had a transit visa instead of a permanent visa, I was an object of suspicion to the French authorities. I was required to go every month to the prefecture, where I stood in line for many hours with thousands of others, to have my *recipissé* (permission to reside in France for one month) renewed. Joe's situation seemed hopeless, and indeed more than a year elapsed before we were allowed to marry. Meanwhile we wasted an inordinate amount of time battling the bureaucracy and getting nowhere.

In August 1938, we moved from the pension where we had first stayed into an apartment in the Sixteenth Arrondissement. Joe and I for the first time were living together openly. This was no problem as far as my friends, European or American, were concerned, but I had to decide what to tell my family. My brother Nelson, ten years older than I, to whom I was greatly attached although I had never confided in him, visited that summer. When I told him that Joe and I were "living a married life," he delighted me by exclaiming warmly: "That's great! That's wonderful! I'm so glad." It made me very happy that Nelson and Joe liked each other at once. When my other brother, Edward, came through Paris soon after, I found it a little easier to tell him, although we were much more different in character and in our values than were Nelson and I. I believe my sister, Ruth, would have accepted my relationship with Joe. But Edward was, except for my mother, the most conservative and conventional member of the family. He had rather Victorian codes about women and was sometimes bossy about his sisters and what he expected of them. However, he only looked serious and said nothing at all, perhaps figuring that, as the damage had been done, reproaches would be of no use. But when I told him I thought I should write my mother that Joe and I were living together, he practically ordered me not to do so. Although at the time I would have preferred to have everything out in the open, I had to admit that Edward was probably right. I wrote home only that Joe and I were engaged.

Our stay in Paris was a period of tension—for Joe in his work and for me in my efforts to help our refugee friends by accompanying them to consulates and by writing endless letters of appeal. We were all restless. Feeling that Pups needed more activity and more companionship with boys and girls his own age, I took him to a camp at Étretat in Normandy run by the American School in Paris, in which I had already enrolled Connie for the coming school year. Connie and I, after visiting Pups at the camp, went to Agay in the south of France for our yearly seaside holiday.

When I had left Vienna in June, I believed I could return occasionally to maintain contact between the comrades in Paris and those still in Austria. Now, although I knew I could not go back to Vienna, I could not completely give up my hope of getting to Austria. A plan began forming in my mind; when we returned to Paris and I talked it over with Joe, he agreed it was worth trying.

I would travel to London on my British passport, in the name of Muriel M. Gardiner, taking with me my birth certificate and my certificate of divorce from my English husband, Julian Gardiner. I would apply for the legal right to use my maiden name, Helen Muriel Morris, and would then get a brand-new British passport in this name.

In September Connie, Fini, and I went to London, and I took the necessary steps to effect a change of name. It was not too complicated, but because one of the requirements was to give notice in the *Sunday Times* for two or three consecutive weeks, I had to remain in London a little longer than I had planned. I did not mind this delay. I was happy to see my English friends and to revisit my favorite spots in London; I loved taking Connie to the zoo, which I had known and enjoyed the summer I was eight years old; and it was an agreeable change to be away from the frustrations of our life and work in Paris. One could not, of course, get away from the political tensions that hovered over all of Europe.

I remember very well my last afternoon in London. Auge and I sat drinking tea in one of London's beautiful parks, reminiscing about the past and wondering about the future. The sun was shining on the majestic trees, still glistening from a recent shower, on the sheep grazing innocently in the fresh grass, and on the happy, peaceful, equally innocent-looking people. I had an already nostalgic feeling that this was to be the last time I would look on such a sunny, peaceful scene. War clouds were gathering; it seemed that any minute the storm might break. Actually, it was to be almost a year before war was declared, but this hour of sunshine lingers in my memory as a farewell to a precious tranquillity about to disappear forever.

I returned to France, pleased with my new passport, in time to bring Pups to Paris a few days before his parents arrived from Turkey to take him home. Although I was sorry to part with him, I was relieved to know that he was with his parents and that all were soon in safety in the United States.

Connie, who had attended the Montessori School in Vienna until leaving in March, now began second grade in the American School in Paris. It was an excellent school, the only one, I believe, which Connie completely enjoyed of the many she attended before going to college. For two months during the winter I took intensive courses in gynecology and obstetrics in two Paris hospitals, and for having completed them I received two certificates, both made out to "Monsieur Gardiner." I also learned a good deal about French medical care indirectly, by accompanying refugee friends to hospitals and clinics. And I devoted spare hours to studying American medical books, preparing to take my examinations in the United States at the first opportunity.

Much of my time, however, was spent going with refugees to consulates and travel offices, to the prefecture and other French administrative offices. I was also kept busy writing to American and English friends, begging for more affidavits and assistance for refugees. My chief pleasures were walks in the woods or horseback rides with Connie and meetings with Ania Herzog, my only close friend in Paris. No matter how sad and disheartened we were, Ania and I always found something to laugh about. It was a great loss to me when Ania and her mother emigrated to Mexico. But we wrote each other frequently, met occasionally in the United States, Mexico, or some other country, and were still able to laugh together as long as Ania lived.

Joe was always busy at the Austrian Socialist office in the rue Trudaine. I occasionally lunched with him and some of the comrades or had them to our apartment on a Sunday. I had difficulty persuading our frugal maid Hélène to prepare enough food for guests and usually had to tell her that there would be two or three more than were really invited. Once, when Leichter dropped in unexpectedly at lunchtime and I was trying to stretch the obviously insufficient meal, he passed back his three-quarters-full coffee cup to me, saying, true to form: "Would you mind filling this up? I have a tic; I can't drink coffee except out of a full cup." In spite of my discomfiture, I found his frankness rather endearing.

But I had other matters on my mind: our friends in Austria. The Socialist comrades there had been told by their leaders to remain Socialists but to discontinue their previous political activities, which, under the Nazi regime, would have meant risking their lives without being in any way effective. Apart from having to contend with the essential changes effected by the Nazis in Austria itself, there was another problem, little known except to those immediately involved—the difficulty of establishing contact between the leaders in exile and the comrades in Austria. My new passport was to come in handy in this regard.

Twice I went to Switzerland for a few days to meet Pav, one of our Socialist comrades who had remained in Austria but who, as a sports reporter for a Berlin newspaper, had permission to travel. It must have been in October that we met in Saint Moritz, for I remember the glorious golden color of the trees in the mountain sunshine. We exchanged information and I gave Pav instructions from the party in exile. First and most important was to emphasize that our comrades in Austria were to undertake no illegal activity. Most of them were known to the police, including of course Pav himself. I did my utmost to persuade him not to return to Austria and passed on to him again all the arguments Joe and his closest colleague, Podlipnig, had repeatedly given him. Pav promised several times that he would remain abroad "the next time," after marrying his fiancée and bringing her with him, but he always returned to Vienna.

I had known Pav since the Anschluss and liked and trusted him, although I knew that he was occasionally incautious. It was one of the greatest shocks of my life when I learned, at the end of the war, that Pav had become a spy for the

Gestapo. In fact, I was for a long time unwilling to believe that it was so. It did not at all fit with my idea of Pav's character. Only later, when I read in Joe's book *Am Beispiel Oesterreich (In the Twilight of Socialism)* * his analysis of how this transformation must have taken place, could I begin to accept it. I do not believe that Pav's convictions changed; I think he felt that becoming a spy was the only way to save his life. It would be of enormous interest to me to psychoanalyze such a person, or indeed to read a detailed report of any such deep, genuine psychoanalysis, but I do not know of any.

I began to plan my trip to some of the Austrian provinces, coached by Josef Podlipnig, who knew the comrades there and how they should be approached. I was to go first to Klagenfurt in Carinthia, Podlipnig's home province, as it had been Joe's for the eight years before he was exiled to Vienna in 1934. Then I would visit comrades in Salzburg and Linz. Podlipnig gave me the names and addresses of one key family in each of these three cities, together with various code words and sentences by which to identify myself as having come from him. He told me many details of his past meetings with these comrades, which only he and they could know. He described exactly the persons I was to see and instructed me on what to tell them and what information I should bring back. Having a good memory, I had no difficulty retaining all of this in my mind with no need even for coded notes.

I left Paris one November day on a train that would bring me to Klagenfurt early the next morning. I traveled, of course, on my British passport, where I was described as a "student," so I took with me an Austrian guidebook and a couple of books on the history, art, and architecture of the provinces I would be visiting. I had also some sort of small teaching manual in European history.

* *In the Twilight of Socialism* (New York: Frederick A. Praeger, Inc., 1953).

At Klagenfurt, if I remember correctly, I checked my light suitcase at the station, taking with me only my handbag and the guidebook to be sure I would give the impression of being a tourist. At an early hour, I appeared at the home of Herr S., who had a barbershop in the same building. He was alone in the kitchen when I rang the bell. As soon as I had given the code word, he welcomed me with literally open arms. He could not hear enough about Podlipnig and the other friends in exile or talk fast enough to tell me all the news of our Carinthian comrades. He got Ferdinand Wedenig to join us, and together we spent several joyful hours. I had never experienced greater warmth or gratitude than these two wonderful men showed me. I never saw my host, the barber, again, as he died before my first return to Carinthia in 1949. Wedenig, who after the war became governor of the province of Carinthia, spent an evening with Joe and me on every subsequent trip we took to Klagenfurt and always brought me flowers. Although I saw him so seldom, we clearly shared warm feelings of friendship and admiration.

I do not remember all the details of this visit to Klagenfurt. I took a room at a hotel, probably for two nights, and dutifully walked about sightseeing and studying the historical monuments. The next morning I took a train to St. Veit an der Glan, where Joe had lived for eight years, to see his friend Gisela Rauter and deliver political as well as personal messages from him to her and to their mutual friends. I had met Gisela briefly once during my early acquaintance with Joe, when she was spending a day or two in Vienna. I had offered the Lammgasse studio as a place for them to meet and, after welcoming Gisela there, had made her a cup of tea and then left. Now in St. Veit I asked for her at the shop where she was employed and learned that she was at lunch and at what time she would be back. At the specified time I was looking in shop windows nearby and immediately recognized her as she approached. I stopped her before she entered and asked whether she was Fräulein Rauter. I then told her I had messages from "Seppl" (the name all his old friends called Joe) from Paris. Gisela immediately suspected a trap and claimed, very convincingly, that she did not know what I was talking about. I gave her many details, including the Lammgasse address she had gone to, but she was rightly suspicious and had obviously forgotten much about the visit. "I know nothing about it," she said. Then I told her more about Joe and about the Lammgasse, and finally something I said refreshed her recollection. "Did you give me anything to eat at the time?" she asked me, still cautiously. "I gave you only a cup of tea," I replied. "I offered you a meal, but you didn't want anything but tea. Then I left." How fortunate that we had both remembered this! At last Gisela believed me; her face lighted up with joy and she took me inside her office, which she occupied alone. We had a satisfying talk without being disturbed.

I suppose I must have returned to the hotel in Klagenfurt for the night and gone the next day to Salzburg, where I was to see Herr and Frau K. Again I checked my bag at the station and set out for the home of my contacts, a walk of perhaps twenty or thirty minutes along quiet roads where it was easy to see that I was not being followed. It was a beautiful autumn day. My way led through an attractive district on the edge of town with small, typically Austrian houses with gardens, in some of which chrysanthemums were still blooming.

I knocked at the door to one of these houses and Frau K., a handsome woman whom I recognized at once from Podlipnig's accurate description, invited me into the kitchen. However, she did not respond to any of the code words or the many identifying data I produced. I told her exactly where and when Podlipnig had seen her last and certain details of what they had discussed and arranged. She remained cold and unmoved. Her husband sat there too but took no part in the conversation. Now Frau K. began asking me questions: Where was I from, what was my nationality, what was I doing in Austria? I told her that I was British and had been studying medicine in Vienna, where I had worked with the Socialist underground, and that I was now returning briefly to bring messages from the comrades in Paris to a few of those still in Austria. "How can you prove it?" "I have a British passport." "Show it to me." Reluctantly I took out my passport. As a matter of caution I would have preferred that no one know my name, but I felt that to refuse to show my passport would really cast suspicion on me and that Frau K. was quite capable of reporting me to the police. At this point Herr K. came over to examine my passport also and asked one or two questions in a friendly voice. But Frau K. remained adamantly hostile. I suddenly broke down and wept. I did not like crying in front of them, and it certainly did not help my cause with Frau K. As soon as I could control myself, I said good-bye and left, feeling absolutely wretched.

I walked back to the station, having decided to leave for Linz on the first train. As I approached the station, I observed that someone on a bicycle was slowly following me. The street was otherwise empty. I found some reason to pause for a moment so that the rider might pass, but when the bicycle caught up with me I saw that it was Herr K. He gave me a kind and sympathetic smile and said: "I wanted to make sure you got to the station safely. Good-bye." I thanked him and we shook hands. I felt sure that had he seen me alone he would have received me quite differently, but he was helpless in the presence of his domineering wife.

A train for Linz was leaving almost immediately, and I arrived there about five o'clock and took a hotel room. I knew I might have a problem in finding Herr B., the comrade I was to contact in Linz. Podlipnig had given me all the usual information—what tram to take, at what stop to get off, how to reach the street, what the house looked like— with one omission: he could not remember the number of the house. It was either the third or fourth in a row of similar houses. I knew Herr B. worked all day and would be at home only in the evening, but it was now quite dark and I would have preferred to locate the house by daylight and return later, sure of the address. However, this would have meant spending the entire next day and evening in Linz, which I was loath to do. After my unhappy visit to Salzburg, I was eager to return to Paris.

I decided I would follow the directions to Herr B.'s home that same evening. If I could identify the house with certainty, I would go in; if not, I would return to explore the following day. I took the tram as directed. There were not more than two or three other people left in the tram at my stop, which was the end-station, and they quickly disappeared. I easily found Herr B.'s street and the row of houses but in the darkness had no way of ascertaining which house was Herr B.'s. So I walked on, making a little circle through the mostly empty streets, and then returned to the end-station where I took the tram back to the center of Linz. I would have to make the trip by daylight the next day.

Although Herr B. had no telephone, I believed I might find the street number in a directory of addresses at the post office. If not, there might be a name on the door. Failing both of these, I believed that Podlipnig had described the house accurately enough for me to distinguish it from its neighbors. It had to be either the third or the fourth house on the right, and I knew some details that I was sure would identify it.

Back in Linz, feeling certain that I had not been observed on this trip, I sat for a while in a coffeehouse and then, weary and disappointed, I checked into a hotel and went to bed.

I was awakened abruptly by a thunderous knocking on my door. Turning on the lamp, I saw that it was close to six in the morning. The imperious knocking came again. "What is it?" I called out, putting on a dressing gown.

"Geheime Staatspolizei," came the answer. I opened the door. There stood a tall, handsome young man in uniform, who immediately raised his right arm. "Heil Hitler. Geheime Staatspolizei," he repeated and showed me his credentials—a quite unnecessary nicety, since it would never

have occurred to me that he could be anyone other than a
Gestapo agent.

"This is *it*. They've got me now," I thought, with real
terror in my heart. Either I had been followed the previous
evening or on one of my trips to a comrade, or possibly Frau
K. had reported me to the police.

"Your identification, please," said my visitor. I turned back
into the room and spent a minute or two unlocking and
searching through my suitcase, although I knew quite well
that my passport was in my handbag. I needed this minute,
rummaging through my belongings with my back turned to
the officer, to think. I had often pictured—or thought I was
picturing—a confrontation with the Gestapo, but the picture was nothing like the reality. I had not foreseen the
physical aspects—my wildly beating heart, the weakness in
my knees. Nor had I experienced in my imagination the
panic that now overwhelmed me. What should my attitude
be? Indignation? That might irritate my inquisitor. Ingratia-
tion? That would be of no use with this man. I remembered
what my lawyer had told me years before when I had to
appear in a civil court case in Chicago: "Answer all questions politely but briefly; never offer more information than
asked for; never ask a question unless there is something
you have not understood." I thought I should follow that
advice now. I handed the officer my British passport without
a word. He studied it.

"Your occupation?"

"Student."

"What do you study?"

"History, languages, and art."

"What are you doing in Linz?"

"Sightseeing."

"Why in Linz?"

"It is an interesting city historically."

"Have you ever been here before?"

"No."

"Do you know anyone here?"

"No one."

"How long are you staying?"

"A few days, depending on how interesting it is."

"When did you arrive?"

"Yesterday afternoon."

"What did you do yesterday?"

"Rested, walked around a little, and had supper in a coffeehouse."

"You speak German very well."

"I have studied it a long while."

After another dozen or so such questions, the young man finally gave me back my passport, saluted once more, and left.

When I went downstairs I stopped to speak to the clerk at the desk. I felt that indignation would be appropriate here, and I might get some clues by questioning him.

"That was a nice visitor you sent me at six this morning," I said. "Do you always allow a stranger to go up to a guest's room unannounced?"

"What do you mean? What visitor?"

"The Gestapo man. Waking me up at six in the morning! Didn't he check with you first? You could at least have telephoned me, if there was any reason for him to see me. That's no way to run a hotel."

"Oh, God, were they here again? The idiots! They make these spot checks every few weeks. They just walk in and go to whatever rooms they please. Pay no attention to them."

"Didn't he check with you first?" I repeated. "I thought he might have been looking for foreigners."

"No. They just do what they please. The tourists always complain. We've had to get used to it."

"I thought Austria was trying to encourage tourists," I said, still showing irritation. "This is bound to keep them away. Do they pick on this hotel particularly?"

"No, no, all the hotels complain. But there's nothing we can do."

Somewhat reassured, I went to a coffeehouse and ate a

large breakfast. I had learned, early in my illegal work, that
at times of stress eating was a real help, and fortunately I
was always hungry. Then I began my sightseeing, with
guidebook and history book in hand, always looking out for
anyone who might be following me. Churches were particularly favorable for losing a follower, since most had several
entrances. I wandered all over the city and satisfied myself
that no one was watching me. In the late afternoon, but
while it was still daylight, I dared to go out to Herr B.'s
neighborhood and easily identified the house. I kept on
walking in the fortunately almost empty streets until I came
to an obscure coffeehouse, where I settled down with my
books and a newspaper, had a light supper, and sat reading
until after dark, when I felt sure Herr B. would be home
from work.

Herr B. welcomed me with evident pleasure as soon as I
had given the first indication of having been sent by his
friends in Paris. He took me into the kitchen, where his
wife and two children were clearing away the evening meal,
and introduced them to me. We all sat down together to
talk. I was surprised that the parents spoke so openly in the
presence of the children, who were perhaps ten and eleven
years of age, without even a word of caution to them. I knew
that the Nazis were already encouraging children to betray
their parents and were even rewarding them for doing so. I
was touched by the complete trust and harmony in the B.
family. We told each other everything we could, and when
I finally left, it was with the sorrowful feeling of parting
from old friends.

Strangely, I do not remember leaving Linz, nor whether I
left late that night or the next morning. I know only that
the many hours in the train before reaching the border seemed
absolutely endless. I was relieved but too exhausted to feel
even gladness when I was safely out of Austria. Almost eleven
years were to elapse before I would see Austria again. When
I did return, I learned from Lore, at that time living in Salzburg, a little more about Herr and Frau K. After the An-

schluss Herr K. had become a member of the NSDAP, the Nazi German Workers Party, in order, he claimed, to conceal or disguise his anti-Nazi beliefs. His claim was presumably a true one, since he remained friendly and helpful to all his former Socialist friends and was later arrested and imprisoned by the Gestapo. While he was in prison, however, Frau K. behaved hatefully and threateningly to a number of these friends. After the war, Herr K. returned from prison and joined the Austrian Communist Party. He worked in a union, as he had done before. Later he came into conflict with the Communist Party leaders and was expelled from the party. He then rejoined the Socialist Party and was a respected functionary in Upper Austria until he died at age sixty-one. Frau K. has since died also.

During the winter of 1938–39 we several times met Austrian friends who had been politically inactive during the illegal period. Joe had acquired a "safe-conduct" travel paper from the French government, which allowed him to make two legal trips, in his own name, to Switzerland. We went with Connie and Fini to Saint Moritz to ski during Connie's Christmas holidays. Then she and Fini returned to Paris and Joe and I went for a few days to Davos, where we met the Bohmers and Albin, another old friend of Joe's. We had arranged to stay at the same hotel but let it appear that we had met the Bohmers and Albin there for the first time; then, after a day or two, we requested to have our meals at the same table. It was a very happy and relaxing time. Our friends could give us news from Austria and take back a few messages to other friends. I have already mentioned meeting Kaethe Gutherz in front of the Zurich post office in March 1939. This tactic functioned perfectly, and Kaethe went on with us to Arosa for a few days. This was just at the time that Hitler, in Prague, proclaimed the dissolution of the state of Czechoslovakia. Of course we were all pretty gloomy.

Joe and I had made no progress in our attempts to get permission to marry. Since there seemed no prospect of succeeding in the near future, I decided to go to the United States without him in order to take my New York State medical examinations, which would be given in late June. I was afraid I would forget the little medicine I knew if I waited any longer. So, as I needed some experience in American hospitals to learn the terminology and become more familiar with American medicine before taking the exams, I left Paris in late March 1939, taking Connie, Fini, and our little dog, Klecks, with me.

The last time I had been in the United States was in 1933. I was happy and excited now, as the ship pulled into the harbor and slowly docked. But I had had no idea what a welcome I would receive! Although it was late in the evening, a group of close friends—Margaret, Gladys, Kay, Betty, Helen Furnas, Margarita Konenkov, and others—were waiting for us on the pier. I was overwhelmed with joy and gratitude.

Helen had found us very suitable rooms in a small apartment-hotel near Washington Square. I was able to do some work at the Beth Israel Hospital, not too far away, and get some tutoring from one of the young doctors there to familiarize myself with American medical vocabulary and the kinds of questions likely to be asked. Connie attended the City and Country School, within easy walking distance. I was happy to be with my old friends again and to see more of my sister, Ruth Bakwin, and her family. She had four children, close to Connie in age, and Connie spent time with them in New York and at their country home in Westchester. Visiting them was a pleasure in itself, and later I had a special reason to be glad that Connie had an affectionate relationship with her Aunt Ruth and Uncle Harry and their children.

The medical boards were difficult, and of course I did not learn the outcome for months. I felt I had done poorly on "medicine." One important question with several detailed subheadings was about hay fever. I knew at once that I had failed this question utterly. Hay fever was unknown in Europe, I had not read about it in any of the American books I studied, and I had never thought of it as a "disease." I did indeed fail the exam in medicine but passed the others, so I would have to take only that one again, the next time the examinations coincided with my presence in New York.

I had been spending a good deal of time with my lawyer, who was also a good friend, exploring all conceivable ways for Joe and me to marry. We considered everything, even the possibility of getting Joe onto an American ship (perhaps one cruising in the Mediterranean) where we could be married according to United States law, since we would be on American territory. But all the "possible" solutions turned out to be impossible. However, sometime in June, Joe cabled me that his papers had been put in order and that we could marry in August.

Right after my examinations Connie and I visited my mother at our Wisconsin summer home, and then, in mid-July, sailed on the *Normandie* for France, accompanied by Gladys, who had agreed to be a witness at our wedding.

It was France's former Socialist premier, Léon Blum, who had made our marriage possible, but there was still considerable red tape to be cut through before we could actually marry at the Mairie of Paris's Sixteenth Arrondissement on the first of August. A member of the American consulate attended; Gladys Lack and Bob Casey, an archaeologist friend who happened to be in Paris, were our two American witnesses. The only other "guests" were Connie and Fini and Kathia and Friedrich Adler. We all had a happy luncheon together before we scattered in various directions. Gladys returned to the United States. Bob Casey left Europe only after the outbreak of the war, on the British steamship *Athenia*, which was torpedoed at sea. Mercifully Bob was saved.

Fini took a vacation, perhaps in England. I believe it was at this time that she married Tony Hyndman and thus became a British subject. However, she returned to Paris to be with us a few weeks longer.

Joe, Connie, and I went to Juan-les-Pins for a pleasant,

quiet vacation, our last in Europe for many years. Joe had obtained an immigration visa to the United States so we booked passage for the three of us to New York on a British ship, to sail on September 6.

We returned to Paris about August 17. Hitler's obvious intention to occupy the free city of Danzig and his flagrant belligerency had changed the prevailing dread of war into justified consternation. I thought war was imminent and that Paris might be bombed without warning. I sent Connie to a camp in Normandy run by the owners of the American School she had attended. A number of the teachers and children she had known were there, and she was happy among old friends. I felt that, whether war came or not, the grim, depressive atmosphere of Paris was bound to be harmful to a child.

A week later the Hitler-Stalin nonaggression pact was announced. Joe and I, alone at home, heard it on the radio. It was something I had never foreseen or imagined. I wept. I had believed myself free of any illusions about the Soviet Union, but I must still have had some lingering belief that Communism was not so appalling as Nazism. Now the two had practically become one.

On the other hand, I believed that there might now be less danger of an immediate world war. How could France and England, which had been appeasing Hitler up to this point, stand up against Germany and Russia together? It did not make sense to me. I soon discovered how wrong my passionate trust in logic and reason could be!

All Paris was preparing for war. Most foreigners who could do so were leaving. Gas masks were in great demand; so was dark cloth for blackout curtains, as well as paper tape to glue across the windows in order to prevent their shattering. Forces were being mobilized; taxis and most buses were confiscated for military purposes. Joe and I went out and bought two bicycles. On one of the last days of August I insisted that Fini go to England. I don't remember how we got to the railroad station—I suppose by subway. I do remember very well practically fighting our way through the panicky crowds at the station and Fini at last getting up the steps of the overflowing train. It was still more difficult for me to get her two heavy suitcases up to her, and I succeeded only as the train began to pull out.

I had told Hélène, our maid, that I thought she should go back to her family in the south of France, and she had left a few days earlier. Joe and I were alone. Would war come before we were to sail for America? And, even if it did not, would Joe be willing to leave our comrades? We knew nothing. We could only live from day to day—more literally from hour to hour.

War actually broke out on September 1, when Hitler attacked Poland. On Sunday, September 3, Joe went early to the office in the rue Trudaine, and I decided to occupy myself cleaning the kitchen. It is strange how, in a period of suspenseful waiting, it seems necessary to involve oneself in some simple manual task. (I felt the same need many times later, while waiting for a report after a friend's operation, for instance; and Joe and I both reacted in this way in July 1956, while anxiously awaiting news of Connie, in her ninth month of pregnancy, and her husband, Harold Harvey, who were on the sinking *Andrea Doria*. Both of us cleaned and tidied the house for four hours until we learned that they were safe.) This Sunday morning in 1939, as I was scrubbing the kitchen floor, Joe telephoned me from the office that France and England had declared war.

However, our ship did not sail on September 6. Joe could not, in any case, have sailed then. All German- or Austrian-born men in France were immediately ordered to present themselves for internment, most of them at the Paris football stadium, "Colombes," on Monday, September 4. They were to take with them toilet articles, a few pieces of clothing, a blanket, and food for several days. Joe wanted to take some reading matter also, and I gave him my one-volume complete Shakespeare. Preparations had to be made hastily. "Little" Otto Bauer's wife and their two younger children were visiting in Switzerland and of course could not now return. Otto was concerned about leaving Poldi and Rosi, now about seventeen and sixteen years old, alone. I asked the girls to stay with me, and they moved in that Monday before their father and Joe left with their knapsacks for the stadium. It was a sad moment for us all.

What was our surprise when, at about six o'clock, Joe and Otto reappeared at the apartment! They had stood in line for hours trying to get themselves interned, but—as so often happened with French bureaucracy—nothing had functioned. Thousands of men stood all day in a line that scarcely moved, until not only they but also the officials at the desks registering them were exhausted. Only a small number of men had been admitted; the rest were told to return the following day. Again the same thing happened; Joe and Otto were back with us at six. Only on Wednesday, the day Joe and Connie and I should have sailed from Europe, were they actually interned in the stadium, under miserable conditions. There they remained for a week or so until they were transported to a "camp" at Meslay, some hours from Paris, where the conditions were even more miserable—an open, muddy field, at first without even tents, surrounded by barbed wire.

There was much for me to do during these early days of war. Connie was my first preoccupation. I was thankful that she was not in Paris, with the air-raid sirens sounding day and night, forcing us to take refuge in the basement of the apartment house or—if on the street—in the nearest air-raid shelter. I was unwilling to leave France while Joe was still interned but wanted to send Connie to my sister in the United States as soon as possible. The family of my friend Gladys Lack had a travel agency in Paris, and I was well acquainted with John, the manager, a friendly, efficient man, who had often been helpful to me. Now I turned to him to try to get a place for Connie on the first available American ship. There were few ships and thousands of stranded tourists were waiting for accommodations. Connie, a British subject, had her American visa, but it was necessary to get a French exit permit. I had seen a notice that the American Legion (an organization I had always rather looked down on, although Nelson was an enthusiastic supporter of it) would help Americans and their dependents in obtaining exit permits, so I took Connie's and my passports and also Joe's travel documents to them. I had little hope that they could get an exit permit for Joe, an "enemy alien," but it was worth trying. Within only a few days I picked them up, all three stamped with exit permits. Presumably the American Legion had some arrangement with the relevant French ministry to stamp all the documents of American dependents without individual scrutiny. I felt a surge of gratitude and warm affection for the hitherto disdained American Legion.

Very soon I went to Étretat, the first of several visits, to spend a day or two with Connie. We talked everything over. Connie asked many questions about the war and about Joe's situation. When I explained why I wanted her to go to New York to stay with her Aunt Ruth, Connie listened carefully and asked more questions. She did not protest, although she could not have been happy at the prospect of leaving Joe in camp and me in Paris and traveling alone in wartime. Besides talking seriously, I was able to do some pleasant things with Connie: walking along the heather-covered cliffs, picking blackberries in the September sunshine, swimming in the sea.

We Socialists had all been shocked that the anti-Nazi refugees had been rounded up and interned together with the Nazis, but many of us still hoped for some future differentiation and possible release of the proven anti-Nazis. A few of the Austrian Socialist leaders, Julius Deutsch, Karl Hans Sailer, and Oskar Pollak, had not been interned. They carried on the work at the office in the rue Trudaine and even brought out the party journal, the *Kampf*, against the decision of the interned majority of the Austrian Socialist Board in Exile. I hoped that these three who had escaped intern-

ment would have some influence in freeing the others, but
weeks passed without anything being accomplished. I turned
to a few persons who I thought might possibly be of help in
Joe's case.

The first person I visited was my Aunt Blanche, whom I
knew to be in Paris at the Ritz Hotel. Uncle Frank, my
grandmother Morris's younger brother, had married Blanche,
a woman much younger than himself, so I had a great-aunt
by marriage younger than my parents and my other aunts
and uncles. When Uncle Frank died, not long after my father's death, my mother took Aunt Blanche with her two
children, about my age, and their "Mademoiselle" into our
home for a year. I was good friends with the children and
got on well enough with Aunt Blanche, though I always
thought her a rather superficial woman. Later she married
an Italian marchese and sometimes when I was in Rome
invited me to elegant dinners or parties at her beautiful palace overlooking the Tiber. I must have seen her a few times
in Paris; in any case I knew she was friendly with several
persons of influence in the French government. Aunt Blanche
was not one to whom I would naturally have turned for help,
but I thought my mother's hospitality and great kindness to
her family in a time of need might give me a certain claim.

Aunt Blanche received me in her hotel suite, we exchanged a few words about the discomforts and inconve-
niences of Paris in wartime, and then I told her Joe's story
in detail. I believed that since Joe was a prominent anti-
Nazi and had an American wife, a visa, and an exit permit,
it should be possible to persuade the French authorities to
release him from camp and allow him to leave at once for
the United States. Aunt Blanche listened attentively, and
when I had finished she said in a burst of enthusiasm: "I
can help you, Muriel. I know I can help you. I know just
the right thing to solve your problem. Wait a moment." She
disappeared into another room and returned shortly with
her arms full of booklets and printed matter. "Take these,"
she said, loading the papers into my arms. "These will com-

fort you; these will direct you in this difficult time. They have given my life meaning, no matter what hardships I have gone through; and they will do the same for you." One glance showed me that they were Christian Science tracts and literature! I never saw Aunt Blanche again.

The other person to whom I turned for help was in every respect a complete contrast to Aunt Blanche. Before I had left Vienna, Austrian friends had given me an introduction to Madame Hanne Benzion, an old friend of theirs from the Sudetenland who, after studying and working for some years in Vienna, had married a French writer and journalist and was now living in Paris. I had been a little wary of introductions of this sort and furthermore had been too busy in Paris to look up Madame Benzion. Now it occurred to me that her French husband (I knew practically no French people) might be able to give me advice. My first meeting with Hanne was a great experience; I knew I had found a friend. She and her husband gave me much more than advice; they gave me sincere love and understanding. I think my only happy day that fall was the day I went with Hanne to Ville D'Avray and we walked under the trees around the lovely lake that Corot so often painted. This outing crystallized our friendship, which has grown deeper through the years.

Letters reached us from Joe, Otto, and others in the camp at Meslay describing the misery. "We anti-Fascists," Joe wrote me, "who were received in this democratic country as political exiles, are now treated exactly like the German Fascists in France, as 'enemy aliens.' We are all here together. There were no tents when we arrived and we had to sleep a whole week long on the wet grass of a meadow. Now we have tents, but they are too small to house us all and of too poor quality to protect us against wind, rain, and the increasing cold. We lie on the hard ground, on our sides, one next to the other like sardines in a can. Some have no blankets. We are all constantly hungry and also thirsty. We have not enough water even to drink, let alone wash, brush our teeth, or shave." And in another letter: "A whole week of rain has turned the ground into an ocean of mud, into which our feet sink deep on the way to the food center or to the open pit which serves as a toilet."

These letters sometimes made me cry from pity and anger. But another letter from Joe brought tears to my eyes for quite a different reason. It was a single page, and I thought and still think it the most noble and beautiful letter I have ever received. For this reason, I cannot forbear quoting it, though it is well known to all lovers of Shakespeare:

> When, in disgrace with fortune and men's eyes,
> I all alone beweep my outcast state
> And trouble deaf heaven with my bootless cries,
> And look upon myself, and curse my fate,
> Wishing me like to one more rich in hope,
> Featured like him, like him with friends possessed,
> Desiring this man's art and that man's scope,
> With what I most enjoy contented least,
> Yet in these thoughts myself almost despising,
> Haply I think on thee, and then my state,
> Like to the lark at break of day arising
> From sullen earth, sings hymns at heaven's gate,
>> For thy sweet love remembered such wealth brings
>> That then I scorn to change my state with kings.

When I tried to get sleeping bags for our friends, I could find only two in the whole city of Paris. Poldi said she could make some, using our sewing machine, so I bought waterproof material and warm cloth for lining, and Poldi and Rosi made a half-dozen sleeping bags, which we mailed to Joe and Otto and others.

I wanted to visit the camp, in the hope not only of seeing Joe, but also of talking with the camp commander and showing him Joe's documents with visa and exit permit. To travel to Meslay, however, one had to get a special safe-conduct paper, to obtain which required much time and many trips to various government offices. I finally succeeded and set out by train for Le Mans, the railroad station from which I

would have to take a taxi the few remaining miles to Meslay. I had filled a knapsack for Joe with warm underclothing
and socks, a sweater, a second pair of shoes, foods such as
chocolate and dried fruits, and vitamins and a few medica-
tions.

In the train beside me sat a young woman, carefully holding a cardboard box which appeared to be from a pastry shop.
We fell into talk and found we were both going to Meslay,
where our husbands were interned. My neighbor then ex-
citedly told me her story, with many tearful interruptions:
she was a Frenchwoman who had married a German busi-
nessman working for a respected firm in Paris. It had apparently never occurred to either of them that her husband
might be in trouble when hostilities broke out. She simply
could not understand it. Today was her husband's birthday—she was sure she would be allowed to see him on this
important day and give him the birthday cake she had had
made for him. At this point she opened the box and showed
me a dainty little cake, with her husband's name and *Joyeux
Anniversaire* elaborately traced in pink letters on the white
icing. I myself was almost ready to weep, so touched was I
by this young woman's innocence and naïveté. How would
her husband, hungry, cold, and mud-covered, react when he
received this carefully prepared gift that would be devoured
in five minutes? Would he understand her solicitude for his
happiness, showing itself in this artless way, or would he
curse her, at least silently, for not bringing him a warm
sweater or blanket?

We took a taxi together from the station at Le Mans through
country roads to the camp. Our driver had some difficulty
finding the entrance gate in the barbed wire. When we finally found it and told our errands to the sentry on duty, he
said he would convey a message to the commander. We
waited for perhaps fifteen minutes, in what appeared to be
in a wilderness, enlivened only by barbed wire; we could
see no persons and no sign of a camp.

At length an officer came limping down the path and talked

to us through the gate. I recognized him as the commander from the descriptions in Joe's letters of an elderly man of stern countenance, grizzled hair, and a severe limp. No, it was impossible to see or talk with any internee, even through the gate. No, not even on one's husband's birthday. No, the commander had nothing to do with anyone's release, even to go to America; that depended on other authorities. This was final; the commander had no more time to listen. Yes, we might leave the knapsack and birthday cake; he would try to have them distributed at mailtime the next day. He could not help it if the birthday had passed. Good-bye.

We drove back to the station, my little companion still weeping, and took the train back to Paris.

My safe-conduct, which I had had such difficulty procuring, had never been looked at. It was good for a whole week, and this gave me an idea. I could go once more to Le Mans, a large industrial town, and there buy fifty or more blankets and take them by taxi or truck to Meslay to be distributed among our shivering friends. This thought comforted me. I went the next morning to the office in the rue Trudaine to report on my visit to the camp and on my project for getting blankets to our comrades.

Deutsch received me at his desk with a cheery smile. I eagerly began to describe my plan to buy and deliver the blankets, but he interrupted me, smiling still more broadly. "That won't be necessary; it's already been arranged. We have bought a truckload of blankets and hired a truck to deliver them to the camp." I was surprised and delighted, but a little skeptical as to how long this might take. "That's fine," I said, "but how soon can you get them there? I could go right away if there's any problem." "No problem," Deutsch replied with evident satisfaction. "They will go today or tomorrow, and with them several crates of lemons; the men need vitamins." My skepticism was appeased; somehow the lemons were a convincing touch. When I inquired a few days later, and then a week after that, I was given evasive answers. Apparently no one except Deutsch, either in or out of camp, had ever heard of the blankets or lemons, and they were never received. I am still angry and baffled by this heartlessness. Is it possible that the blankets and lemons were a pure fabrication of Deutsch's, simply to prevent someone else from getting the credit for a humane deed? This is hard to believe, but what other explanation is there?

My family and friends in America were of course concerned about me and kept writing and cabling me to come home. These cables caused me endless trouble because of the red tape involved in receiving them. A notice would be sent to me that a cable addressed to me had arrived in Paris. I had to take this notice and my identification to a particular office to get written permission to receive the cable. This office was always crowded, and one had to stand in line sometimes for an hour or more and fill out certain forms before getting the permission. Then it was necessary to take this form to the post and telegraph office some distance away and again stand in line. If the cable required an answer, one had to repeat the same performance: go back to the office that granted permission to send the cable, then return to the post office to do so. Often one cable and reply took a half-day, and if I found another notice upon my return home, the entire day might be used up. After too many such fruitless days, I cabled my lawyer in New York asking him to request my family and friends not to cable me unless it was absolutely necessary.

Poldi and Rosi were a great help to me; they were pleasant company, helped with the marketing and cooking, took Klecks out for walks, and were able to take care of many things. Transportation in Paris was so slow and sporadic that I traveled almost everywhere by bicycle, even around the Étoile, which I dared to do because there was little traffic.

At last John, in the Lack Travel Office, secured passage for Connie on an American ship to New York. Connie would have a berth in a cabin for four, in which two other clients of the Lack office were also booked. One of the women, whom I met briefly, kindly promised to keep an eye on

Connie. The ship would sail from le Verdon, the port of Bordeaux, in early October, but dates were uncertain. Connie might have to wait in Bordeaux. Through an acquaintance I met an American man, a teacher, going on the same ship, who agreed to travel on the train with Connie and see that she got a hotel room in Bordeaux if they had to wait there.

In late September I fetched Connie from the camp in Normandy and brought her to Paris for a day or two. Her passport was in order, she had ship and train tickets for herself and Klecks, who would accompany her, travelers' checks, and plenty of reading matter. We left the apartment early one morning on foot, hoping to get a taxi. I carried Connie's suitcase; she was leading Klecks on a leash. When we had walked for five minutes a car stopped beside us and a young man stepped out offering to give us a lift. We were very grateful to be taken to a taxi. At the train we met the American teacher, a pleasant person in good spirits, and I felt reasonably comfortable leaving Connie with him. Both he and Connie wrote me reassuring letters from Bordeaux. I had confidence that Connie would manage the trip well and keep her equilibrium no matter what fears and discomforts she experienced. But I took a deep breath of relief and joy when I received my sister's cable that Connie was with her, safe and sound.

I can do no more than mention the negotiations and intrigues that were taking place among the various groups of Austrian emigrés. Representatives of the French and British governments, seeking to form an Austrian government in exile, were trying to bring together Socialists, monarchists, Austro-Fascists, and various other groups, including a small, self-styled "Social Democratic Group" (which had nothing to do with the Socialist Party) led by "Hermann," a former member of the Funke group who had left the party. Deutsch and Sailer both became involved in these intrigues, although they did not agree with each other. Deutsch finally took the stand that he could make no decision without the agreement of the members of the Austrian Socialist Foreign Board, who were still interned. One week later, on about October 20, Joe, Otto Bauer, Podlipnig, Leichter, Manfred Ackermann, and Hubeny (a younger member of the Socialist Foreign Board) were released from camp. Joe made it clear that to accept the invitation to become a part of the official Austrian Committee, "an invitation to work together with paid agents for reactionary political goals," would mean the end of the Foreign Board. He would never take part in the committee, and the majority of the Foreign Board, including Leichter and Ackermann, supported this position. This was why an Austrian government in exile was never formed. Joe recommended that several members of the board try to leave France, where the authorities, in their propaganda against Hitler, would not allow the Austrian Socialists to pursue their own political goals. Joe believed that they should go to the United States, England, or Sweden, where they might at least have more freedom to express their aims. The board approved Joe's going to the United States, which indeed had already been agreed to before the outbreak of the war.

Joe and I were fortunate in securing a tiny cabin to ourselves on the S.S. *Manhattan*, scheduled to sail about mid-November. It was, I believe, the last American ship to leave France. Determined to take a minimum of luggage with us, I set about disposing of our furniture and other belongings. We gave our friends clothes and useful household articles and left our piano with Ackermann—who, of course, had to abandon it with his other possessions when, about six months later, the refugees fled Paris. Everything else was packed in trunks and boxes and, together with our furniture, was stored in the Paris warehouse of the reputable British firm Wheatley and Company. I left money with John, of the Lack Travel Office, to pay any necessary bills. At the end of the war we found that everything had been confiscated by the Nazis, "because they had no proof that we were not Jews." I deeply regretted the loss of letters, personal papers, and photographs, of a few pictures painted by friends, and of several beautiful works given to us by our friend the Russian sculptor Sergei Konenkov. None of these things could have the same meaning for anyone else that they had for us—but they were not living things and deserved no tears.

We left Paris on an Indian summer day in November for Bordeaux, where we found we would have to remain at least overnight. Actually two or three days passed, incredibly slowly, before we were told that the boat train for le Verdon would leave early the following morning. We piled out of the train at the dock to find an enormous crowd already there; the ship must have been booked far beyond its normal capacity. The entire closed-in dock area, stifling on this extraordinarily hot day, was swarming with pushing, excited people of various nationalities, all with their bags, bundles, and boxes. By roping off a small area, a not too successful attempt had been made to form a queue in front of the tables where the authorities sat to examine documents and hand out boarding passes. I don't remember what happened to our suitcases, but I know I was dripping with perspiration and my arms were aching from carrying my winter coat, a raincoat, and my suit jacket for the entire day.

In due time our turn came to approach the authorities. At the first table were civilian officials to examine the passports. At the next sat an elderly French general, tired and sweating in his heavy uniform with its stars and ribbons. He was flanked by two lesser military men. I was in front of Joe. My passport was carefully examined, a few routine questions were asked, and I proceeded to the table of the general, who, after a cursory glance at my passport and exit permit, handed me the precious boarding pass, a small orange-colored cardboard square with a few printed words. I stepped ahead, waiting for Joe, who by this time had been cleared by the passport official and was standing in front of the general's desk.

"You cannot leave France," barked the general. "You are an enemy alien."

"But I have permission from the French government to leave, and the passport controller has found my papers in order."

"The military is the final authority," replied the general.

A long discussion followed, quiet and polite on Joe's side, loud and angry on the general's. The waiting crowd was becoming impatient. Finally the general thrust the document back into Joe's hands. "Come back when I have finished with all the others," said the general, signaling for the next person to take Joe's place.

Joe and I looked at each other in despair. What were we to do? Although we had in the past year become a little more used to the idea of "tipping" someone to do us a favor, bribery in this case was certainly out of the question. How were we even to get through this long day of waiting? We had reached the dock at about ten in the morning; it was now twelve or one, but the crowd seemed not to have diminished at all. Strangely, I cannot remember getting anything to eat or drink, yet I do not remember hunger or thirst either—only heat, weariness, worry, and the noisy mass of people. As darkness approached, I realized that the crowd was at last thinning, and we found a place to lean our weary bodies against a wall. We did not talk much, but I am sure we shared the same thoughts: how unbearable to be held back at this last minute! I would have been ready to plead, weeping, to the general, but I was convinced it would be useless; he looked implacable.

It was late in the evening, at least twelve hours since our arrival, when Joe was able to go to the end of the line of the last dozen or so people. The dock and ship were of course completely blacked out, with only a few shaded lamps on the desks and one at the gangplank. I stood in a dark corner nearby, waiting in horrible suspense.

Joe later described this final interview to me. While the general was still occupied with the last persons in the line and his two younger assistants were preparing to close up, Joe spoke to the nearer one. "Although I was an Austrian,"

Joe told him, "I fled to France and gave up my Austrian citizenship because I am a fervent anti-Nazi. I am a writer and journalist, as you see"—Joe pointed to his travel papers, on which his occupation was described as writer—"and I want to go to the United States to write articles against the Nazis and make propaganda for the side of France and England in this anti-Hitler war. I can be very useful to France once I am in the United States." This argument appealed to the assistant, who spoke persuasively to the general when Joe's turn came. "All right, here's your pass. Do all you can for France," said the weary general.

Joe and I boarded the ship together.

Epilogue

During our first two years in the United States both Joe and I were busy with refugee work. When in the spring of 1940 the Nazis invaded France and were about to occupy Paris, the French, with admirable humanity, opened the gates of the internment camps and allowed the German- and Austrian-born refugees, along with many who had already been released to serve in "work battalions," to flee with thousands of French citizens to the unoccupied south of France. Nevertheless these refugees were not out of danger, and most were of course without work or means of livelihood.

Joe, together with our friend Karl Frank, who had been a leader of the German Socialist underground group Neu Beginnen, was instrumental in persuading President Roosevelt (largely through the energetic intervention of his wife, Eleanor) to grant emergency visas to about two hundred of the most endangered German and Austrian refugees then in the unoccupied French zone. As a result of obtaining these visas, a large number of our friends arrived in New York on the Greek ship *Nea Hellas* in September 1940. Others came later. I was kept busy finding them rooms, a task by no means easy at that time. Joe and I were also in frequent contact with the International Rescue Committee, as well as with other committees.

Many of our friends needed medical care. My sister, a physician connected with the New York Infirmary for Women and Children, was helpful in getting free medical and dental services for the women and children. I often accompanied them to their first appointments, and I took a number of men to various clinics or hospitals. Eventually most of the families found homes and work, some of them in New York. For several years we often had refugee families living for a few weeks or months in our New York apartment, among them Joe's younger brother Loisl—now calling himself Louis—with his wife and year-old son, who had arrived from England in 1941, and, the next year, the Friedrich Adlers.

Nearly as soon as we had arrived in America, Joe began collecting books and articles about Central Europe, most of which we bought from German refugees. Many were rare and very valuable; some were works the Nazis had ordered to be burned. Later, we obtained Austrian books also and expanded the collection to include history, philosophy, and other aspects of Central European life. Joe at first needed the books for his own studies and writing, but within a short time we opened the library to serious students who could not find such material elsewhere. Years later, when Joe went to Vietnam, he collected an equally important library—mostly in French and English but partly in Vietnamese—which was probably the best in the United States. Our books and the many students who wanted to use them were crowding us out of our good-sized apartment, so we asked Felix Augenfeld to look for a brownstone house, two floors of which he could remodel into library stacks and study carrels. He happened upon a twenty-four-foot lot, for sale at a very low price since it had been vacant, being between larger buildings, for many years. Auge built us a most beautiful and functional house-library, with a separate top-floor apartment for Otto Bauer, who had become our librarian, and his wife and daughter. We had always intended that the collections should go eventually to some large library or university. About 1970, when we were thinking of giving up the house, two perfect solutions presented themselves. Carinthia, the only province in Austria without a government university, was building one in Klagenfurt and gladly accepted our German-Austrian collection. Soon after this, Harvard University invited Joe to come to Harvard to meet with their librarians and heads of the various departments of East Asian Studies and advise them how to build up a library for a new Department of Vietnamese Studies. Joe, delighted to attend the meeting, told them the beginning would be very simple: they should simply accept our collection. We were as pleased as they. A dinner was given for Joe, attended by many Harvard dignitaries, and it was a most joyful occasion. Several people spoke in tribute to Joe, and he in reply gave one of his best and wittiest speeches.

During our first two years in the United States, I was working twice a week as a psychiatric consultant in two New York nursery schools and had supervision about two hours a week by Berta Bornstein, an outstanding child analyst. I then took a year's rotating medical internship in Trenton (near the New Jersey home we had acquired, while still keeping our New York apartment), finishing in 1943 and following which I had intended to take a psychiatric residency. But as there seemed a chance that as soon as the war ended I might go to Europe to do refugee work there (I did not know what kind of work or with what organization), I thought I needed some experience in public health. Furthermore, I did not want to leave Connie again at this time or to live in a hospital for another year. I therefore took a job in the New Jersey Department of Health as assistant medical director and field-worker in the Bureau of Venereal Disease Control. To my surprise, I liked it very much and learned a good deal. After a year and a half of this work, I was asked by the International Rescue Committee to go to France as their Western European supervisor. I flew in an army plane to Paris in early April 1945.

My work there—building up a committee to help the many refugees already in France (most of them German, Austrian, or Spanish) and, after the war in Europe ended in May, the thousands more being released from German concentration camps—was sad and difficult, but it turned out to be the beginning of an excellent and very worthwhile committee which has continued to function to the present day. Our friend Hanne Benzion served as manager for many years.

I went to Paris with the understanding that I would remain there not more than six months. I returned to the United States in September 1945, on an American troop ship, the *Santa Rosa*, carrying about four thousand people, ten times more than the four hundred it had been built for. I was one of only twelve women aboard—most of them nuns, who, with their voluminous garments, took up an unduly large share of our cramped quarters—housed in what had probably been a two-bed cabin but was now crowded with four rows of narrow three-tiered cots. We were served two meals a day, one at 6 A.M., the other at 3 P.M., in the "officers' mess," a small room with a counter and stools. All the rest of the day I stood—there was no place to sit—crowded shoulder to shoulder with the American soldiers. I listened with fascination to the tragic, sometimes comic, and often abhorrent stories of their war experiences. Most of these young men were good-natured, pleasant, outgoing, happy to talk to an American woman, perhaps for the first time in years. As they poured out their stories, I learned firsthand that many of them—not too unlike the Germans, Russians, and other soldiers—had stolen, vandalized, and raped. Some admitted that they had, in cold blood, shot their enemies approaching with raised arms to give themselves up. I realized that persons of natural integrity can become cruel and selfish under certain circumstances, as when corrupted by war. But I learned also of acts of great generosity, courage, and self-sacrifice. I believed, more strongly than before, that one cannot, should not, make sweeping generalizations about any nation.

Soon after my return to New Jersey that fall of 1945, Joe went abroad for several months to continue the work I had begun in Paris. He returned the following year and was able, with a few members of other refugee organizations, to travel to Austria and Germany, under the protection of the American army. This trip to Europe meant that Joe had to interrupt his work on a book about Austrian Socialism in the 1930s and his activities as leader of the illegal Socialist party. Eventually he finished this first book in German. It was published in Germany, then translated and published in America under the title *In the Twilight of Socialism,** and later published in France. It caused a great deal of controversy in Austria, since many Austrians, including some of our comrades, thought it disparaging and one-sided; others found it the best book that could possibly have been written on the subject.

This is perhaps the place to say a few words about Joe's later career, in which both writing and refugee work played an important part. At home he continued studying and writing, usually about various aspects of socialism. He had prepared and written the greater part of two books, neither of which was ever completed, when the International Rescue Committee again called for his services, this time for a new and very different task. At the end of the French-Indochina War in 1954, when Vietnam was divided into two sections, a free and peaceable exchange of persons between North and South was allowed. Many people coming from North Vietnam to the south had no families, no homes; some were children or young students, and there were of course a number of intellectuals and artists, the type of refugee that the International Rescue Committee had always made special efforts to assist.

Joe spent several months in Saigon that year, organizing a committee there to help refugees find homes and work. From the beginning Joe loved the Vietnamese people and was deeply interested in them and in their political situation, but he knew very little of Vietnamese history. He had not been able to find any book in English, and nothing really satisfactory in French, to give him the background he wanted.

*New York: Praeger, 1953.

Before leaving Vietnam, he determined to write, as he said, "the book I wished I could have read." From this time on, through the end of America's war with Vietnam, Joe's thoughts and activities were devoted chiefly to events in that country. He wrote a detailed and scholarly history in three thick volumes,* several smaller books, and a number of articles about Vietnam. He also gave many lectures and made public speeches on the subject. He returned twice to Vietnam, once in 1958 and again in the spring of 1971.

Joe wrote one other book in the late 1960s, which was published later. From the time the two oldest of Connie's and Harold's children began to beg, "Grandpa, please tell us a story," he had told them a continuous tale about a little elephant, Manko, and his animal friends who lived on the Fantasian Continent. All six children (the oldest just seven when the youngest was born) and the friends they often invited to share these delightful adventures were so enchanted that they kept urging "Grandpa" to write them down until he finally complied.** Although the Manko stories are completely different from his previous political books, bits of Joe's political thinking and philosophy crept into them, in such a discreet way as to add to, rather than lessen, their interest. Joe's last writing was his autobiography, the first part of which has been published in German.†

In late 1956, after the Hungarian Revolution, the International Rescue Committee asked Joe and me to go to Vienna, where the refugees who were able to escape were being received. Joe left immediately. My principal work at this time was part-time consulting in schools and teaching two three-hour seminars, each meeting one afternoon a week, at Rutgers, New Jersey State University. I had to make arrange-

*The Smaller Dragon (New York: Praeger, 1958), and Vietnam: A Dragon Embattled, 2 vols. (New York: Praeger, 1967).
**Manko of Mankoland, 3 vols. (New York: Exposition Press, 1977).
†Ortswechsel (Frankfort: Verlag Neue Kritik, 1971).

ments with Rutgers to miss a few of these seminars. The university was obviously proud to have me go, and readily gave permission. So I was in Vienna from the beginning of a fairly long Christmas vacation until early February, when most of the refugee work not yet completed could easily be handled by other committee members. During the following year our New York apartment was again crowded with refugees. We became good friends with one couple (the man had been for a short time Socialist mayor of Budapest) and their lovely eight-year-old daughter.

In following years, Joe received many honors, and I too was honored several times. We received a large medal inscribed to us both from the Hungarian Freedom Fighters, whose headquarters was in Washington. The International Rescue Committee presented Joe with a beautiful plaque (they would have liked to include me, but Joe had done so much more for them that it gave me more pleasure that he alone should receive it). South Vietnam honored him also for his work there.

What made me happiest, and Joe also I am sure, were his honors from Austria. First the government gave him Austria's Great Golden Cross of Honor—the highest honor anyone could receive. We went to Vienna for this occasion and many of Joe's old friends and comrades were present. Some years later the new university in Klagenfurt gave Joe, who had spent his most productive years before going to Vienna in Carinthia, its first honorary degree of Doctor of Philosophy. This was the university's first ceremony and Joe was the only person to receive this honor. All Joe's friends who gathered there were proud of their old comrade, who had achieved so much in spite of having attended school for less than six years.

In 1980 word came to me that the Austrian government wished to give me the Austrian Cross of Honor, First Class. (There are three classes, or possibly four, though not even First Class is the equal of the Great Golden Cross of Honor.) They asked whether I would come to Vienna to receive it

directly from the government or if I would prefer to go to
the embassy in Washington or the consulate in New York.
I chose New York since I was very fond of Consul Nowotny
and since more of my friends could be present there. I found
there was some difficulty in giving a name to the honor I
was about to receive. (In the Vienna Medical School we spoke
of a *Verlegenheitsdiagnose*—an "embarrassment diagnosis," given when we were not sure what a patient's disease
really was.) The first rumor was that it would be "for Science and Art," the second, "for Research and Letters," but
the final wording on the leather box containing the beautiful
cross on the Austrian red-white-red ribbon was "for Letters
and Arts." The title was of little importance to me. I knew
it was a recognition of my dedication to freedom.

I must return to our earlier years in the United States.
Connie's love of nature and animals, which I shared, although not quite so passionately, and her wish to live in the
country had begun to influence my thinking. Connie's con-
stant reiteration, "Mum, *why* do we have to live in New
York? Why can't we live in the country?," made me begin
to ask myself the same question. In June 1940 this wish of
my determined daughter was suddenly fulfilled in a way
that seemed nothing short of a marvel. We had several times
in the winter and spring enjoyed a weekend in the country
home of my friend and lawyer, Wolf Schwabacher, who owned
one half of a large two-family house in Pennington, New
Jersey; Wolf's brother owned the other half. Both families
were there only in summers and occasional weekends since
they had permanent residences in New York.

One Monday in June I went to Wolf's office on some legal
business and found him rather depressed, not at all his usual
cheerful self. The brother who owned the other half of this
home, with separate entrances but under the same roof,
wanted to sell his part immediately. Wolf and his family,
not inclined to stay on with strangers, had reluctantly decided that they also must sell.

"Would you like it if we bought your brother's half?" I asked impulsively. All details were promptly settled; we bought the brother's house, with a half-interest in the caretaker's house, the barn, and other outbuildings, and about two hundred acres of fields and woodlands, at what now seems an unbelievably low price. On Friday of the same week we moved into our "real home," Brookdale Farm, complete with linen and tableware, food and drink, and—best of all—a couple who served as housekeeper and caretaker. A hot dinner was ready for us that very first evening. All this we owe to the Schwabachers' friendship, but even more to Connie's determined character.

Connie went to school because she had to. The rest of her time, when she was not reading, was largely devoted to watching, catching, and caring for wild animals. She fenced off one quarter of her bedroom and covered the linoleum floor with two hundred pounds of sand, which she had persuaded Joe, in one of his weak moments, to steal from the neighboring golf course (his only theft since the hunger period of his boyhood, when he had sometimes stolen an apple or a few potatoes from a farmer's field). This part of her room was the home of thirty box turtles. The walls were lined with aquariums containing wild mice, rats, snakes, water turtles, and some "store" animals that well-meaning friends had given her: an alligator, a black and a white mouse with their pretty, often spotted descendants, and dozens of hamsters. In the center of the room was a large squirrel cage with two little squirrels, which Connie had taken from a treetop nest containing four young squirrels (Connie would never have left the parents without at least two children).

To make room for this menagerie, Connie had taken her bed apart and stored it in a shed. She spent most nights in the woods or the barn, but in bad weather she would lay out her sleeping bag on the floor of her room, squeezing herself in among the books, shoes, and jackets strewn around. We had two rules: Connie had to take a shower and wash her hair before school every morning and she had to care for

her animals and clean their cages. (She was sometimes able
to bribe Joe with ten cents or a quarter to wash the aquariums.)

However, there was a time when Connie's unconven-
tional room presented us with a problem. Joe and Connie
had become United States citizens in February 1943. Immediately thereafter Joe initiated proceedings to adopt Connie, wishing her to be his legal daughter as well as step-
daughter. A pleasant young woman from the adoption agency
visited me at Mercer Hospital, where I was doing my medical internship. After I had dispelled her initial misgivings
upon learning that I, like the other interns, earned twenty-
five dollars a month, and that Joe, a self-employed writer,
was earning nothing at present, she seemed satisfied with
what I told her about Joe and our home. A few days later
she visited Joe, who was alone at Brookdale Farm. After an
agreeable conversation with him, the adoption agent said
she would like to look at Connie's room. Joe, describing this
scene to me, told me how his heart sank; he was convinced
that all was lost. He led the way upstairs and opened the
door to this little zoo. The woman stared in silent amaze-
ment for a full minute. Then, turning to Joe, she asked, "Is
it *always* like this?" "I'm afraid it is," he replied lamely. "I
think it's perfectly wonderful!" was this astonishing woman's comment. "I've never before known parents to let a
child have her room exactly the way she wanted."

Connie completed high school at sixteen. I had insisted
that she prepare for college, but she would be free to choose
whether or not she wanted to go. She was in any case going
to have a free year after high school. We were all in Europe
in the fall of 1947, and planning to remain into the skiing
season, when an old duodenal ulcer of Joe's (owing to his
inadequate diet in postwar France and Italy) revived. Joe and
I decided to return to America, but two Swiss families we
knew offered to keep Connie with them. Connie, who scarcely
knew them, was hesitant. Then, to my surprise, this girl
who had disliked school so much that she had crammed her

last three school years into two, asked me, "Couldn't I go to school in Europe this winter?" I searched through Swiss catalogues of boarding schools and was convinced that Connie, who had enjoyed so much freedom, would never be happy in any of them. Then one day in the French consulate in Rome I caught sight of a poster for the University of Grenoble, which offered intensive courses in French language, literature, and history. This seemed the right place for Connie, so she enrolled immediately.

After two semesters at the University of Grenoble, Connie received a certificate to teach French, then took a summer job at a children's camp in German-speaking Switzerland. She returned home a few weeks before going to McGill, the college of her choice.

Connie completed her four years at McGill and spent the next winter at Sun Valley, working evenings at a hotel and skiing during the day. The two following years she had a job as a substitute teacher in the elementary school of Sun Valley's neighboring village, Ketchum. In spring 1955, she returned to Pennington and New York.

Harold Harvey often spent weekends with us in Pennington. Connie liked him and he was fond of her but had seen little of her since she was sixteen. Now they fell in love and soon married. The next April or May they went to Austria for spring skiing, then to Corsica to camp on the beach and enjoy the swimming and spear fishing. They planned to fly home in July, but as Connie was in her ninth month of pregnancy no airplane would take her. Instead they sailed on the *Andrea Doria.*

Joe had gone to New York on Thursday to meet the ship due to arrive early Friday morning. Late Thursday evening the Swedish ship *Stockholm* rammed a huge hole in the *Andrea Doria.* It was immediately clear that the *Andrea Doria* would sink. I learned of the accident Friday morning at six o'clock and called Joe. I cancelled all my patients— one of the only two times I ever had to do this. More than four anxious hours passed before we received a cable: "Safe

on *Ile de France."* Connie and Harold would arrive that
evening. I drove into New York; then Joe and I met them
at the dock.

In spite of our pass and the cable, we were kept with the
waiting thousands roped off on the pier while reporters, pho-
tographers, and TV men delayed the passengers to get their
story. I had deliberately worn a conspicuously bright dress,
and we found places bordering the open passage. The first
persons coming off the ship near where we stood were Connie and Harold. We slipped under the rope, and I held Connie in my arms. Their clothes were stained with oil and
Connie was barefoot. (Since the crowd on the sinking ship
was bottlenecked at the one rope ladder, while empty life-
boats waited around, Connie and Harold had jumped into
the water and swum to a lifeboat.) Both were smiling. "Hello,"
said Harold, "what's new?" I was smiling and crying. "What's
the matter, Mum?" asked Connie, genuinely surprised.
"Didn't you get our cable?" They were first off the ship
because some humane official, seeing that Connie was close
to delivery, had asked her, "Are you going to a hospital?"
Harold mendaciously answered yes, and they were escorted
past the reporters and into an elevator down to the waiting
crowd. There was of course no luggage to struggle with, our
car was parked nearby, and we were soon on our way to
Pennington on this extraordinarily hot evening of July 27,
1956. Safely home, we all had a good, cooling swim in the
pool. Joan, the first of Connie's and Harold's six children,
was born exactly three weeks later. The parents had, as usual,
been playing tennis the evening before.

The Harveys built a house between Pennington and Trenton with an office for Harold, who practiced medicine there
and in Mercer Hospital. In 1959 they moved to Aspen, where
they had bought a house the preceding year when we were
all there during Christmas vacation. They already had three
children; three more were born during the next few years
in Aspen. Connie became a certified teacher in the ski-school
and taught for many years. Later Harold occasionally taught

also, and all the children were excellent skiers from an early age.

It turned out that Harold, foreign-trained, was not allowed to take the state board examinations in Colorado. At first Connie, and I also, believed he would be dissatisfied and that they would move to another state. But there was so much for both parents to do—raising the children, making repairs and additions to the house, and learning to run a good-sized cattle ranch they had bought, almost adjacent to Snowmass before it became a resort—that Harold soon appeared happy with this different and busy life. Perhaps his twenty years of active medical practice had satisfied that particular need in him, though he always continued to keep up with his profession.

As the children grew older, Connie took over managing the ranch and bought another, larger one near Steamboat Springs, where the children often helped her. She has been deeply involved in preserving the land and the wilderness and in all environmental matters.

In 1946 I finally took my year's psychiatric residency at the State Hospital at Marlboro, New Jersey. I enjoyed this work more than anything I had done before. The fact that I had already been analyzed and had completed most of my theoretical training in psychoanalysis gave me a tremendous advantage in understanding and working with patients, and many of the other residents and staff psychiatrists asked me to teach them what I could. Until then I had been a student most of my life; now I was full of confidence in the work for which I knew I was qualified and well suited.

After my residency I worked a year as psychiatrist and director of four clinics. I then completed my psychoanalytic training at the Institute of the Philadelphia Association for Psychoanalysis. At first I practiced analysis full-time, then combined my practice with teaching at the Institute, at various hospitals and social agencies, and at Rutgers Graduate School of Social Work and Rutgers Department of Education. Some years later I discontinued private practice to work as a psychiatric consultant, first in the public schools of Bucks County, Pennsylvania, and then for the State Department of Education in New Jersey.

Since this work was more flexible and gave me more free time than practicing analysis had done, I was able to undertake a few other projects. I put together and edited a book about the Wolf-Man, containing Freud's and Brunswick's case histories, the Wolf-Man's *Memoirs* and his *Recollections of Sigmund Freud,* and a few chapters by myself.*

I took part in a study of homicides committed by juveniles, which involved visiting young offenders in prisons and reformatories. I became so interested that for years I worked in several prisons as a volunteer psychiatrist with a small number of inmates. It was heartbreaking work since I could do so little to help these patients. I wrote a book of the histories of ten of the young offenders I had known, *The Deadly Innocents: Portraits of Children Who Kill.***

The work I found most gratifying of all was in the public schools. I regarded it as something approaching preventive psychiatry, which appealed to me more than attempting to remedy damage already deep-seated. I liked the contact with children, from kindergarten through high school, and with their parents, who were often desperately seeking help. Most of the teachers, the school administrators, and the special-service personnel wanted both to help the children and to learn all they could. The work was educational as well as clinical. I could make good use of all I had learned in my long years of study and training, and this was deeply satisfying. I loved my work.

Indeed I loved not only my work but life itself. I had many interests and many satisfactions, greatest of all the joys of deep and lasting friendships—in which I include my love

The Wolf-Man by the Wolf-Man (New York: Basic Books, Inc., 1971).
**New York: Basic Books, Inc., 1976.

for Joe, Connie, Harold, and our six grandchildren, for every one of them is a friend as well as a member of the family. Nor do I regret that I have had my share of grief and sorrow, of anxiety and danger. I am proud and happy to quote the following paragraph from a letter I received from Anna Freud, dated October 30, 1972: "I had received the *Philadelphia Bulletin** with the articles in your honour and I was terribly interested to read them. I had not known of the intensity of your political activities in Vienna, only the vaguest rumours, and I was quite fascinated, even a bit envious. I like my own life very much, but if that had not been available and if I had to choose another one, I think it would have been yours."

*The Bulletin of the Philadelphia Association for Psychoanalysis, June 1972, containing among others a brief paper by my husband, entitled "Mary," describing my illegal work in Vienna, 1934–1938.